COLLOQUIAL
PERSIAN

COLLOQUIAL
PERSIAN

By

L. P. ELWELL-SUTTON
B.A. Hons. Arabic

ROUTLEDGE & KEGAN PAUL
BOSTON, LONDON, HENLEY AND MELBOURNE

First published 1941
in Great Britain by
Routledge & Kegan Paul Limited
9 Park Street
Boston, Mass 02108, USA
39 Store Street
London WC1E 7DD
Broadway House
Newtown Road
Henley-on-Thames
Oxon RG9 1EN and
296 Beaconsfield Parade
Middle Park
Melbourne 3206
Australia
Reprinted 1943, 1946, 1952, 1957
1960, 1965, 1971
Reprinted and first Published as a paperback 1975
Reprinted as a paperback 1976, 1979 and 1982

Printed in Great Britain by
T. J. Press (Padstow) Ltd
Padstow, Cornwall

ISBN 0 7100 4327 9 (c)
ISBN 0 7100 8083 2 (p)

CONTENTS

		PAGE
PREFACE	. . . .	vii
INTRODUCTION	. . . . . .	viii
THE PERSO–ARABIC ALPHABET	. . .	1
PRONUNCIATION.	. . . . .	2

LESSON

I. NOUNS, ADJECTIVES, SIMPLE SENTENCE CONSTRUCTION 9

II. PRONOUNS, PREPOSITIONS, INTERROGATIVES, INDEFINITE PRONOUNS 15

III. THE VERB, STEMS, SIMPLE TENSES, VERBAL SENTENCES 23

IV. PARTICIPLES, AUXILIARIES, IRREGULAR VERBS, ADVERBS 30

V. AUXILIARIES, IMPERSONAL AND CAUSATIVE VERBS, SUMMARY OF TENSES . . . 39

VI. COMPOUND VERBS, CONJUNCTIONS . . . 46

VII. SUBORDINATE SENTENCES 51

VIII. NUMERALS 58

IX. TIME, DATE, MEASURES, ETC. . . . 64

X. WORD FORMATION : (a) PERSIAN . . . 70

XI. WORD FORMATION : (b) ARABIC . . . 75

XII. GREETINGS, OATHS, HONORIFICS, POLITE PHRASES, ETC. 82

		PAGE
CONVERSATIONS		89
Travelling		89
Sightseeing		90
Shopping		92
Domestic		94
Office		95
An Investigation		97
At Work		99
In Camp		101
VOCABULARIES		103
A. *English–Persian*		
Military, Naval and Air		103
Technical		106
Professions and Trades, etc.		108
Commercial, Office, etc.		109
Political and Administrative		110
Domestic		112
Clothes		113
Plants and Flowers		113
Animals, Birds, Fish and Insects		114
Parts of Body		115
Proper Names		115
General		117
B. *Persian–English*		127
BIBLIOGRAPHY		139

PREFACE

IT is only in recent years that Western eyes have begun to look with close attention at the extensive (though not thickly populated) country of Iran. Though for many it is still the country of Haji Baba, of Persian carpets and Persian cats, yet there is a growing realization among careful students of foreign affairs that the new Iran is a portent of some significance in the Middle East of to-day. In part this is due to its strategic importance, in part to its importance as an oil-producer, but more, perhaps, than anything, to the new outlook with which its whole social system is permeated. This new outlook, outwardly so strange to the East, and yet in reality derived from something fundamental in the Iranian character, affects every aspect of Iranian life—their politics, their economic system, their culture, their language.

This manual is intended primarily for those whose interest lies in learning to speak the language, and who lack either the time or the ambition to master the apparently bewildering script. It will, however, be useful also for those who intend to go on to the written language. It is designed to cover the language of the common people and no more ; polished speech can, indeed, only be acquired after a study both of Persian literature and of the Arabic language.

My special thanks are due to Dr. J. Heyworth-Dunne and Dr. Bernard Lewis for advice and suggestions, and to my wife, who patiently undertook many of the more arduous duties involved.

INTRODUCTION

THE book is divided into three parts. The Grammatical section is intended to take the student through all the elementary grammar that he will require for colloquial purposes. He should work through these lessons in turn, the exercises of which are designed to provide practice in the subject matter of each. The Conversations, on the other hand, are classified under such topics as travelling, domestic, etc.; they are intended to improve the student's command of vocabulary and colloquial expressions. Full Vocabularies are also provided with the aid of which the student will be able to make up his own sentences or to carry on conversations with native speakers.

Two points are to be noticed. The exercises and conversations have not been literally translated, but an equivalent colloquial English version has been given. The student will find it useful to study the different modes of expression used in Persian and in English.

The system of transcription has been devised to combine, as far as is possible, accuracy, simplicity, and consistency. It does not correspond at all closely with the Arabic alphabet, and therefore probably will not please the scientifically minded; but it is felt that any elaborate system of diacritical points and signs would be not only confusing but quite unnecessary for the purpose for which this book is designed.

THE PERSO-ARABIC ALPHABET

1. The following table gives the Arabic letters used in written Persian and the transcription used in this book. In the third column is given, for comparison, the standard transcription as used in St. Clair Tisdall's *Persian Conversation Grammar*.

Consonants

ا	'	'	ر	r	r	ف	f	f
ب	b	b	ز	z	z	ق	gh	q
پ	p	p	ژ	zh	ž	ک	k	k
ت	t	t	س	s	s	گ	g	g
ث	s	ş	ش	sh	sh	ل	l	l
ج	j	j	ص	s	ş	م	m	m
چ	ch	ch	ض	z	ẓ	ن	n	n
ح	h	ḥ	ط	t	ṯ	و	v	v
خ	kh	kh	ظ	z	ẓ	ه	h	h
د	d	d	ع	'	'	ی	y	y
ذ	z	ẓ	غ	gh	gh			

Vowels

‎َ	a	a	‎ـِه	è	eh	‎ُو	u	ū
‎ِ	e	i	‎ـَا	â	ā	‎َـئ	ê	ai
‎ُ	o	u	‎ـِی	î	ī	‎َـوْ	ô	au

1

PRONUNCIATION

2. Persian contains the following twenty-two consonant sounds :—

(i) Pronounced very much as their English equivalents, care being taken to articulate them fully :

b, f, j, m, p, z.

s—always as in " sit ", never as in " as ".

n—generally nasalized before g and k. Before b and p it becomes m.

h—must always be pronounced, e.g. noh̲sad " nine hundred ", s̲h̲ah̲r " town ".

z̲h̲ [1]—" s " in " pleasure ", or French j in " je ".

s̲h̲ [1]—as in " wis̲h̲ ".

c̲h̲ [1]—as in " c̲h̲eese ".

(ii) The following differ slightly from their English equivalents :—

d, t—rather softer than in English.

l—must be enunciated very clearly, as in " leaf ", even at the end of a word. The English tendency to " swallow " it (hall, bowl, real) must be avoided.

r—must be trilled ; it is always pronounced, e.g. c̲h̲ar̲m " leather ", not c̲h̲ām.

k, g—have their English equivalents before â, o, ô, u (see para. 3) ; before a, e, ê, i they are " palatalized ", that is articulated much further forward in the mouth, the effect being as if a very short y-sound came between consonant and vowel, e.g. kʸetâb " book ", but kâg̲h̲ez " paper ". This rule

---

[1] The underlining indicates that these two letters are to be pronounced as one sound ; it is only used in z̲h̲, s̲h̲, c̲h̲, g̲h̲, k̲h̲. It should be noted that these letters may occur together as separate sounds, in which case they are not underlined, e.g. eshâg̲h̲ = Isaac, c̲h̲izhâ = things (pronounced es-hâg̲h̲, c̲h̲iz-hâ).

also applies when they come at the end of a word, e.g. dôs̱h̲akkʸ " mattress ", sagʸ " dog ".

N.B.—" g " is always hard, as in " garden ", never as in " gem ".

y—clearly articulated ; at the end of a word it sometimes turns into an i- or ê- sound.

v—has a tendency towards w ; at the end of a word it sometimes turns into an ô- or u- sound.

(iii) The following do not occur in English :—

k̲h̲ [1] is used to represent the Scottish and German sounds " ch ". It must never be pronounced as " k " ; on the other hand the opposite extreme of " h " must also be avoided.

g̲h̲ [1] is the " voiced " [2] equivalent of " k̲h̲ " ; it is a " gargled " sound, with something of the quality of the French guttural " r " and of the soft German " g " in " Wagen ". This sound is also generally used for the Arabic " q ", but occasionally, especially at the end of a syllable, something of the Arabic sound (a " k " pronounced deep in the throat) may be preserved (and also even in Persian words). Examples : tag̲h̲sir or taqsir (Ar.) = " fault ", g̲h̲âs̲h̲og̲h̲ or g̲h̲âs̲h̲oq (Pers.) = " spoon ".

N.B.—Doubled consonants must always be pronounced separately ; cf. book̲-c̲ase.

3. *Vowels.*—It is impossible to represent the Persian vowels adequately in transcription ; the system adopted here gives only the main groups and, as in all spoken languages, they vary greatly from dialect to dialect, and even from speaker to speaker.

---

[1] See note [1] on page 2.
[2] " Voiced " consonants are produced by using the voice (the vocal chords) as well as the organs of speech (e.g. the tongue, palate, teeth, etc.) ; thus for example d, b, z are " voiced ", t, p, s are the corresponding " unvoiced " consonants.

a—about half-way between the English vowels "a" in " cat " and " u " in " cut ", with slight tendency towards " e " in " net " ; all these extremes must be avoided. It retains this sound even when followed by r, h, etc.

â—very nearly as the "a" in "wash", but with a tendency towards " a " in " father ". In the Isfahan dialect it is nearer " au " in " Maud ". Before -n it generally becomes u.

e (è in terminations)—roughly as " e " in " net ", or French " è " in " père ", but with a slight tendency towards " i " in " sit " (especially before " y ").

ê—varies from the diphthong " ai " in " maid " to the French " è " in " blè ", but generally has a slight diphthongal tendency—êⁱ.

i—as " ee " in " sweet ", but without the English diphthongal tendency.

o—lies somewhere between the French " o " in " pomme " and " oo " in " foot ", but nearer the former.

ô—varies from the diphthong " ow " in " bowl " to a pure " o " as in the French " mot "—generally "ôᵘ". It frequently stands for " av " or the Arabic diphthong " aw " (" ow " as in " now ").

u—" oo " as in " root " or French " ou " as in " cou ".

N.B.—It should be noted that the above vowels are all distinct in sound, as opposed to length. Each of them may be either short or long, but this distinction has no effect on the sound (and does not in any way correspond to the distinction in the Arabic alphabet). The only rule worth remembering is that vowels followed by two consonants at the end of a word or syllable are lengthened, e.g. hāst = " there is ", gōft = " he said ", sēft = " hard ", nīst = " is not ", etc. In the Isfahan dialect this tendency to " drawl " these vowels is very marked. " ô " and " ê " are also generally long.

This lengthening is not marked in the book, as it would merely create confusion; it can only be picked up with any degree of accuracy by hearing the spoken word, and does not affect the meaning or construction. This, of course, is also the case in English.

Another point to be noticed is that the sound is not affected, as in English, by any following consonant, such as r, h, y, etc. The contrast is shown in the English "charm" and the Persian c̲h̲arm "leather".

(4) The apostrophe ' is used to represent the two Arabic consonants ء (ḥamza) and ع ('ain), as these are not distinguished in Persian. Between two vowels it does not more than separate them, e.g. sâ'at "hour", "watch". Between a vowel and a consonant it indicates a slight slurring of the vowel, e.g. ta'mir "repair" = taᵃmir, fe'lan "actually" = feᵉlan, râje' "concerning" = râjeᵉ, g̲h̲or'ân "Koran" = g̲h̲orᵃân. At the beginning of a word it is not pronounced, and is therefore not shown. Following a consonant at the end of a word it is hardly pronounced, but has the effect of lengthening the preceding vowel in accordance with the two-consonant rule given above (para. 3); e.g. rob' "quarter" = rōb. It is useful to remember that in Arabic the two sounds which this apostrophe represents are regarded as consonants.

Occasionally it is found in purely Persian words, usually between a word and a suffix, e.g. pâ'in = "below".

It must be realized that the printed word can only give an idea of the pronunciation of the sounds of Persian; neither consonants nor vowels correspond exactly to any English sound. Correct pronunciation can only be achieved by listening carefully to native speakers, and imitating or even mimicking their speech.

ACCENT AND PITCH

(5) Generally speaking the accent in Persian is on the last syllable of the word (with the exception of certain grammatical suffixes, such as the pronominal suffixes—see para. 14). It may also occur earlier in the word for the purpose of emphasis, e.g. kard = " he did ", 'nakard = " he did not do " (see para. 26). Frequently there is a secondary accent on one of the preceding syllables, e.g. âshpaz"khâ'nè = " kitchen ".

The most characteristic quality of Persian, however, is the pitch or tone of voice, and it is neglect of this that makes the efforts of most Englishmen ludicrous to an Iranian. It is impossible to represent it satisfactorily on paper even with an elaborate system of diacritical points and signs ; it must be learnt by ear. In this connection a systematic and careful study of the Persian Linguaphone Records would be useful.

DIALECTAL PECULIARITIES

(6) There are numerous dialects in Persian, some of which have been adequately studied. The beginniner, however, would be extremely unwise to attempt to cover all these ; and he will find that the language spoken by the fairly educated classes will be intelligible in most parts. The chief differences are in the pronunciation of the vowels ; the spread of education has meant an increasing standardization in the vocabulary used. There are, however, certain peculiarities used by all classes when speaking to workmen, servants, etc., and even among themselves ; some of these are noted here, and others will be met with in the course of the book.

h, gh, y, v tend to disappear when they come between two vowels, e.g. âghâ " Mr.'' becomes â, miyâyad " he is coming ", miyâd, miravad " he is going ", mirad, mikhâhim " we wish ", mikhim, etc. (see paras. 25, 27).

â before -n (and frequently before -m) becomes u. This is, in fact, the normal pronunciation, and will frequently be used in the exercises without any special explanation. In the vocabularies -ân will always be written, but it may be understood that either pronunciation may be used.

EUPHONY

(7) It frequently happens that the grammatical construction brings together two vowels. In such cases it is usual to insert a " y " for purposes of euphony, though before or after " i " it is not always required (especially in careful speech).

The examples are of two kinds :—

(a) When a word ending in a vowel has a suffix beginning with a vowel.

(i) The Plural ending -ân (para. 9), e.g. âghâyân.

(ii) The Indefinite ending -i (para. 10), e.g. khânè-i or khâneyi.

(iii) The Ezâfè -e- (para. 11), e.g. khânè-ye-bozorg (but not *after* -e-, see (b) below).

(iv) The Pronominal Suffixes (para. 14), e.g. khâneyam (but y is often omitted in this case, and contraction takes place, e.g. khânesh for khâneyesh).

(v) The Present Tense of " budan " (para. 34), e.g. raftè-y-am, raftè-im, or raftè-y-im.

(vi) The Verbal Terminations added to the Present Stem (paras. 25, 29), e.g. miguyam, migu-id, or miguyid, âyandè, etc.

(b) When a prefix ending in a vowel is placed before a word beginning with a vowel.

(i) The Ezâfè (para. 11), which is *never* followed by y, e.g. dôlat-e-irân.

(ii) The Verbal Prefixes mi- and be- (paras. 24, 25), e.g. mi-âvaram, miyâvaram, or miyâram (coll.), beyâyand or beyând (coll.).

(iii) The Negative Prefix na- (para. 26), e.g. nayâyad or nayâd.

NOUNS AND ADJECTIVES. SIMPLE SENTENCE CONSTRUCTION

CASE AND GENDER

(8) THERE are no case inflections in Persian.

There is no distinction of gender, words which are naturally feminine being treated for grammatical purposes exactly as other nouns (e.g. mâdar = "mother", do<u>kh</u>tar = "daughter", "girl", <u>kh</u>âhar = "sister", etc.).

N.B.—In certain words and phrases borrowed from Arabic, the Arabic feminine ending -ah is found, which in Persian becomes -è or -at, e.g. vasilè = "means", forsat = "opportunity". Arabic adjectives qualifying such nouns should strictly speaking take this feminine ending; but in ordinary conversation it is frequently omitted. The Arabic element in Persian is discussed more fully in Lessons X and XI (paras. 70–6).

NUMBER

(9) (i) The ordinary Plural ending is -hâ (in colloquial often -â) ; e.g. ketâbhâ = "books".

(ii) Occasionally the ending -ân (coll. -un) is used for persons, e.g. â<u>gh</u>âyân (pl. of â<u>gh</u>â) = "gentlemen" ; this is the correct use, but is not always observed in colloquial.

(iii) Arabic words very often have the Arabic "Broken" Plural, which consists of an internal change in the form of the word, e.g. <u>sh</u>art "condition", <u>sh</u>arâyet "conditions" ; lâzem, lâzemè "necessary", lavâzem "necessaries" ; serr "secret", asrâr "secrets" (see para. 72).

9

(iv) The Arabic Feminine Plural ending -ât is sometimes found not only with Arabic words (especially those ending in -è or -at), e.g. amaliyât "operations", but also with Persian words, e.g. deh "village", dehât; mivè "fruit", mivejât (note the insertion of -j- after -è, the regular practice with Persian words).

N.B.—Plurals of inanimate objects generally take singular verbs (see para. 28).

ARTICLES

(10) There is no article, either definite or indefinite; the latter is, however, frequently indicated by the suffix -i (unaccented); ketâbi = "a book". In colloquial this is generally strengthened by the use of yek, yey "one", and in this case the -i may even be dropped or attached to yek; yek ketâbi, yek ketâb, yeki ketâb. Notice the use of yek khordè "a mouthful" and yek ghadri "a quantity" in the sense of "some, a little"; yek khordè âb = "a little water".

N.B. (1).—This -i is also often used with nouns qualified by the Indefinite Adjectives (para. 21).

N.B. (2).—This ending is not to be confused with the Relative ending, e.g. esfahâni = "of Isfahan" (which is derived from Arabic), or with the Qualitative ending, e.g. mardi "manliness" from mard "man" (para. 69).

THE EZÂFÈ

(11) A second word may be linked to a noun by the Ezâfè construction, which consists in the insertion of the particle -e- (-ye- after a vowel) between the two words; it has the following uses :—

(i) Possessive (two nouns): ketâb-e-ba<u>ch</u>è = " the child's book "; pesar-e-rezâ = " the son of Reza " (notice also hosên-e-rezâ = " Hosain (son) of Reza "). In colloquial the word mâl " property " is generally inserted as well, e.g. ketâb mâl-e-ba<u>ch</u>è.

(ii) Apposition: hosên-e-na<u>ghgh</u>â<u>sh</u> = " Hosain the painter ".

(iii) Descriptive :—

(*a*) Nouns : râh-e-esfahân = " the road to Isfahan ".
Many compound nouns are formed from two nouns without the insertion of the Ezâfè, e.g. <u>kh</u>âb-gâh = " bedroom " (sleep-place), ruz-nâmè = " newspaper " (day-letter) (see para. 68).

(*b*) Adjectives follow the noun they govern, and are linked to it by the Ezâfè; <u>kh</u>ânè-ye-bozorg = " the big house ". But after an indefinite noun the Ezâfè is omitted, e.g. ba<u>ch</u>è-i-ku<u>ch</u>ek, yek ba<u>ch</u>è ku<u>ch</u>ek = " a small child ".

N.B.—In certain cases the adjective precedes the noun, e.g. pir-e-mard = " the old man ".
They are not inflected in the Plural (unless used as nouns), e.g. <u>kh</u>ânehâ-ye-bozorg = " big houses ", but bozorgân = " great ones ". The Ezâfè construction can never be split, though several nouns and/or adjectives may be linked together by it, e.g. do<u>kh</u>tar-e-bozorg-e-ahmad = " Ahmad's eldest (lit. big) daughter " ; dôlat-e-<u>sh</u>âhan<u>sh</u>âhi-ye-irân = " the Imperial Government of Iran " ; ra'is-e-bânk-e-melli = " the manager of the National Bank ".

N.B.—For other uses (Prepositions, Infinitives, and Verbal Nouns) see paras. 19 and 37.
This Ezâfè link is a very close one, and can never be separated.

COMPARATIVE AND SUPERLATIVE

(12) The Comparative is formed by the addition of the
suffix -tar, e.g. bozorgtar = " bigger ", ku<u>ch</u>ektar =
" smaller ". " Than " is translated by az (lit. from).

The correct form of the Superlative has the suffix -tarin ;
bozorgtarin = " the biggest " ; bozorgtarin-e-otomobilhâ =
" the biggest of the cars ". A commoner colloquial construction is the Comparative with az hamè " than all ", e.g.
bozorgtar az hamè.

" Very," etc., is expressed as in such phrases as the
following :—

<u>kh</u>êli boland   = *very long*
besyâr <u>kh</u>ob   = *very good*
har <u>ch</u>è zudtar = *as quickly as possible* (lit. *whatever (is)*
                              quicker).

Certain words have special forms for the Comparative and
Superlative, e.g. <u>kh</u>ob, behtar, behtarin = " good, better,
best ".

CONSTRUCTION OF SIMPLE SENTENCES

(13) The order of the simple sentence is : Subject, Predicate,
Verb, e.g. hasan hâzer ast = " Hasan is present ". The verb
" is " (described more fully in para. 30) has two forms in
the Present Tense, as follows (3rd Pers.) : ast (in colloquial -è), and hast = " exists ", " there is " ; e.g. ba<u>ch</u>è
ku<u>ch</u>ek-è = " the child is small " ;   âb hast = " there is
water ".

The negative particle is na-, prefixed to the verb ; before
ast and hast it gives the form nist, e.g. hâzer nist = " he
is not present " ; mivè nist = " there is no fruit ".

Inanimate objects in the plural generally have a singular
verb, e.g. ketâbhâ <u>kh</u>êli hast = " there are many books ".

Questions may be indicated (if there is no Interrogative Pronoun—see para. 20) by the tone of voice alone, the word-order being kept; in correct speech the particle âyâ may be inserted at the beginning of the sentence, without any other change. Common conversational uses are :—

(i) The addition of yâ na (= " or not "—accent on na) at the end of the sentence.

(ii) The negating of the verb.

Neither of these is nearly as strong as the English usage, and may be used even in polite conversation.

EXERCISE I

(1) yek ketâb kuchek	= **A small book**
(2) ketâb-e-kuchek	= **The small book**
(3) ketâb kuchek ast	= **The book is small**
(4) shahr bozorg-è	= **The town is large**
(5) mivè-ye-khob	= **Good fruit**
(6) ra'is-e-bânk hâzer ast ?	= **Is the bank manager present ?**
(7) khêr, âghâ, hâzer nist	= **No sir, he is not**
(8) pedar-e-ahmad naghghâsh-è	= **Ahmad's father is a painter**
(9) manzel-e-pesar-e-rezâ boland ast	= **The house of Reza's son is tall**
(10) ketâb mâl-e-eshâgh [1] ast	= **The book is Eshaq's**
(11) otomobil hâzer-è	= **The car is ready**
(12) esfahân shahr-e-bozorg-è	= **Isfahan is a big city**
(13) fe'lan âb nist	= **Actually, there is no water**
(14) âb khêli lâzem ast	= **Water is very necessary**
(15) taghsir-e-hosên ast	= **It is Husain's fault**
(16) naghghâsh hâzer ast	= **The painter is here**

See note [1] on page 2.

(17) zud hâzer ast   = He is early

(18) yek ghadri mivè hast   = There is some fruit

(19) râh khêli boland ast   = The road is very long

(20) rezâ az hosên kuchektar = Reza is smaller than Husain
ast

(21) shahr-e-tehrân   bozorg- = The city of Tehran is the
tarin-e-shahrhâ-ye-irân ast   largest of the cities of Iran
(or: .. az hamè-ye-shahrhâ-
ye-irân bozorgtar ..)

(22) âb kharâb ast   = The water is bad

(23) âb-e-khob hast   = There is good water

(24) postkhânè hast yâ na ?   = Is there a post office ?

(25) balè, âghâ, postkhânè hast = Yes, sir, there is

(26) pedar-e-bachè ghâyeb ast = The child's father is absent

PRONOUNS, PREPOSITIONS, INTERROGATIVES, INDEFINITE PRONOUNS

(14) (i) *Separate.*

	Singular.		*Plural.*	
1.	man	= *I*	mâ	= *we*
2.	tô	= *you*	s͟homâ	= *you*
3.	u (literary)	= *he, she, it*	is͟hân	= *they*
	in ⎫ *		ânhâ* (col.)	
	ân ⎭ (coll.)			

(* Literally " this ", " that ", " those ".)

(ii) *Suffixes.*

	Singular.		*Plural.*	
1.	-am	= *my, me*	-amân	= *our, us*
2.	-at	= *your, you*	-atân	= *your, you*
3.	-(e)s͟h	= *his, him*	-es͟hân	= *their, them*

N.B.—tô and -at are used in speaking to intimate friends, children, servants, workmen, etc. ; in other cases s͟homâ and -atân are used for the singular as well as the plural.

(15) The *Separate* forms are used :—

(*a*) To introduce any sentence in which a pronoun or a reference to a pronoun occurs. Thus they may be used as—

   (i) the grammatical subject of a sentence :

   in tanbal-è = *he is lazy*

   (ii) the logical subject (usually linking with a pronominal suffix later in the sentence) :

   tô manzelat in ast ? = (*you*) *is this your house ?*

15

This use is rather colloquial, and not as a rule found in correct speech, in which the pronouns are replaced by honorifics (see para. 79).

In both the above cases they may be omitted altogerher.

(*b*) Linked to a noun by the Ezâfè to indicate the possessive case, e.g. ketâb-e-man = " my book ". This, however, is rather emphatic, and usually the suffix forms are used (without Ezâfè).

(16) As indicated in the table, the *Suffixes* are used—

(*a*) in the possessive construction (ketâbe<u>sh</u> = "his book ");

(*b*) as the objects of verbs and prepositions (see para. 28).

They are attached to the word (noun, verb, preposition, etc.) with which they are linked and are unaccented. They are used much more widely in colloquial than in correct speech. When the noun is qualified by an adjective, the pronoun follows the latter, e.g. ketâb-e-tâzè-ye-man = " my new book ".

REFLEXIVE PRONOUNS

(17) Especially in colloquial, the separate forms given above are often replaced by the Reflexive Pronoun <u>kh</u>od " self " with a pronominal suffix : <u>kh</u>odam = " myself, I " ; manzel mâl-e-<u>kh</u>odam = " my (own) house " : <u>kh</u>ode<u>sh</u> hâzer-è = " he (himself) is present ".

<u>kh</u>od should always refer to the speaker or to the subject of the sentence. In this way it may be either Possessive or the Subject or Object of a verb.

DEMONSTRATIVES

(18) in = *this*
ân, un = *that*

When used as adjectives, the demonstratives are unchanged in the plural : ân ba<u>ch</u>è = " that child ", in <u>kh</u>ânehâ = " these houses ". When, however, they are used as pronouns, they take the plural ending -hâ ; inhâ = " these (men, things) ", ânhâ = " those, they " (= i<u>sh</u>ân).

They are frequently found compounded with other words, e.g. hamin, -ân = " the same " (ham = " even, also ") ; <u>ch</u>onin, -ân = " such " (<u>ch</u>ûn = " like ") ; injâ, ânjâ = " here, there " (jâ = " place "), etc.

PREPOSITIONS

(19) The prepositions, all of which precede the noun they govern, fall into two groups, those without Ezâfè, and those with Ezâfè.

(i) *Without Ezâfè.*

az	= *from*	bi	= *without*
bâ	= *with*	tâ	= *as far as*
be	= *to, with*	joz	= *except*
tu	= *in* (coll.—also with Ezâfè)	dar	= *in*
		bar	= (*on*—in compounds)

az is often compounded with prepositions of group (ii) : pi<u>sh</u> az, <u>gh</u>abl az = " before (time) " ; <u>gh</u>êr az = " other than, besides ".

be has a great many idiomatic uses, and is frequently used in compounds with other prepositions, e.g. tâ be = " as far as, until " ; be-joz (= " except ") ; be-<u>gh</u>êr az, etc.

bar is rarely used by itself, but is commonly prefixed to such prepositions as sar, ru (see next group) ; it is also found in the compound proposition banâ bar = " according to " ; banâ bar in = " accordingly, therefore ".

(ii) *With Ezâfè.*

A few of these are true prepositions; others are nouns. The remainder are adverbs, e.g. :—

PREPOSITIONS

bedun	= *without*
barâ-(ye)	= *for*
bar(-e) (coll.)	

NOUNS

ru, bar ru	= *on*
sar, bar sar	= *on, at the top of*
jâ, bejâ avaz	} = *instead of*
jehat, be-jehat, az jehat sabab, be-sabab, az sabab	} = *because of*
bâbat	= *concerning*
taraf, be-taraf	= *in the direction of*
be-jâneb	= *by the side of, beside*
be-vasilè be-vâsetè	} = *by means of*

ADVERBS

birun	= *outside*
dâkhel	= *inside*
bâlâ	= *above*
pâ'in	= *below, at the foot of*
zir	= *beneath*

pi<u>sh</u>	
pahlu	= *near, in the presence of,*
nazd, nazdik	*in the possession of,* chez
jolô (we-)	= *in front of,*
pi<u>sh</u>	*before (place)*
po<u>sh</u>t	
a<u>gh</u>ab	= *behind*
meyân	= *in the midst of, between*
bên	= *between*

Most of these prepositions may be preceded by az, dar, tâ etc., with their appropriate meanings, e.g. :—

az birun	= *from outside*
dar meyân	= *in between*
tâ pâ'in	= *as far as the foot of*
be-jolô	= *to the front of*

All prepositions may be followed by the separate forms of the pronouns (with or without Ezâfè as appropriate), but in colloquial it is more usual to use the pronominal suffixes ; e.g. aze<u>sh</u> = " from him ", betun = " to you " (pl.), tu<u>sh</u> = " in it ", a<u>gh</u>abat = " behind you " (sing.), etc. For the first persons, however, man and mâ are used in preference to the suffixes.

pi<u>sh</u> and pahlu are often used in place of the verb " to have ", e.g. ketâb pi<u>sh</u>-e-man ast = " I have the book " ; nân pahluye<u>sh</u> (pahlu<u>sh</u>) nist = " he has no bread ".

INTERROGATIVES

(20) These words may generally be used either as pronouns, or adjectivally in close connection with a noun or pronoun.

They are usually placed as near as possible to the verb, or
verb and qualifying word.

kodâm ?   = *which ?*
ki ?   = *who ?*

chè ?
chè chiz ? } = *what ?*
chi ?

chè tôr
chè jur(è) } = *what kind of ? how ?*
chè gunè

chand ?   = *how much, how many ?* (followed
                 by the noun in the Singular.)

cherâ ?   = *why ?*
kê ?   = *when ?*
tâ kê ?   = *till when ? how long ?*
kojâ ?
ku ?   } = *where ?*

INDEFINITE PRONOUNS

(21) kas, kasi   = *someone*
     hich   = *none* (verb takes na-)

     hichkas   = *no one* (verb takes na-)
     har   } = *all, every, each, any* (N.B.—
     hamè   }   hamesh *all of it, everything.*)
     harkas   = *everyone*
     tamâm-e-   = *all, the whole of*
     digar   = *other, another, more*
     chand (sing.)
     chand tâ (pl.) } = *some*
     chandin
     chandin az
     ba'zi az   } = *some of*

kam	= *few, little*
kami	
yek kami	} = *a few, a little*
yekdigar	= *one another*

When these are used as adjectives, the following noun generally takes the indefinite suffix -i (see para. 10).

EXERCISE II

(1) manzelatun kojâ-st ?— manzelam birun-e-<u>sh</u>ahr-è = **Where is your house ?— My house is outside the town**

(2) <u>ch</u>è tôr hastid ?—man <u>kh</u>êli nâ<u>kh</u>o<u>sh</u>am = **How are you ?—I am very ill**

(3) hasan <u>ch</u>erâ hâzer nist ?— dar bâzâr-è = **Why is Hasan not here ?— He is in the bazaar**

(4) dar zamestân barf <u>kh</u>êli hast = **In winter there is much snow**

(5) â<u>gh</u>â-ye-hakim tu man-zel-è ?—<u>kh</u>êr, â<u>gh</u>â, <u>kh</u>ode<u>sh</u> hâzer nist = **Is the doctor in the house ? No, sir, he (himself) is not present**

(6) â<u>sh</u>paz birun ast ?—na<u>kh</u>êr, â<u>gh</u>â, ham injâ-st = **Is the cook out ?—No, sir, he is just here**

(7) ân <u>sh</u>a<u>kh</u>s ki-è ?—barâdar-e-<u>sh</u>ôfer-è = **Who is that man ?—It is the driver's brother**

(8) in <u>ch</u>iz <u>ch</u>i-è ?—<u>ch</u>izi nist = **What is this thing ?—It is nothing**

(9) <u>ch</u>è <u>kh</u>abar-è ?—in <u>ch</u>è <u>ch</u>iz-è ? = **What is the news, what has happened ?—What (thing) is this ?**

(10) mivè-ye-<u>kh</u>ob tu bâzâr hast yâ na ? = **Is there good fruit in the bazaar ?**

(11) kodâm az inhâ shofer-è ?   = **Which of these is the driver ?**

(12) hîchkas hâzer nist   = **No one is present**

(13) chè chiz ru-ye-miz ast ?——= **What is on the table ?—It** nun ast   **is bread**

(14) in kâghez bar-e shomâ-st = **This letter is for you**

(15) mâshin-e-mâ   kojâ-st ?— = **Where is our car ?—It is on** dâkhel-e-râh (sar-e-râh) -è.   **the road**

(16) velâyatat   ku ?—velâ- = **Where is your home ?—My** yatam esfahân-è   **home is Isfahan**

THE VERB, STEMS, SIMPLE TENSES, VERBAL SENTENCES

(22) THE Infinitive of all Persian Verbs ends in -tan (after ḵẖ, f, s, s̱ẖ), -dan (after n, r, or a vowel), or -idan. From the Infinitive are formed (directly or indirectly) the *two stems* on which the tense system is built up.

(*a*) By cutting off the termination -an, the *Past Stem* is formed, e.g. kos̱ẖtan " to kill ", kos̱ẖt ; mândan " to remain ", mând ; davidan " to run ", david ; ḵẖaridan " to buy ", ḵẖarid ; didan " to see ", did.

The Past Stem is always regular.

(*b*) By cutting off the terminations -tan, -dan, or -idan (as the case may be), the *Present Stem* is formed ; e.g. kos̱ẖtan, kos̱ẖ ; mândan, mân ; ḵẖaridan, ḵẖar.

In many common verbs this stem is formed irregularly, and must be learned from the vocabulary ; e.g. kardan " to do ", kon ; didan, bin ; raftan " to go ", rav ; âmadan " to come ", â ; dâs̱ẖtan " to have ", dâr (see para. 31).

Once these two stems have been obtained, the conjugation of the verb is quite regular.

N.B.—The original root of the verb is the Present Stem. To this was added the termination -dan to form the Infinitive. For phonetic reasons, however, this ending could only be used after a stem ending in r, n, or a vowel. In the case of stems ending in other consonants (and frequently even in cases with r, n, and vowels) one of the following methods was adopted :—

(i) i was inserted before -dan, e.g. dav-, davidan ; ḵẖar, ḵẖaridan. This is very common with roots formed from Arabic words, and from nouns, adjectives, etc. (even when euphony does not demand it). (But note that certain other verbs also end in -idan, e.g. didan).

(ii) After f, s̱ẖ (s, ḵẖ), -dan became -tan, e.g. s̱ẖekâf—s̱ẖekâftan " to split ", kos̱ẖ—kos̱ẖtan.

N.B.—Roots ending in these consonants are comparatively rare, -s and -ḵẖ not being found at all ; but in the Irregular Verbs—(iii)—many *Infinitives* have them as the result of phonetic change.

(iii) A change was made in the final consonant (and frequently in the vowels) of the stem. These are the Irregular Verbs ; a list of the common ones will be found in para. 31, together with a note on the phonetic changes that take place.

(23) The following Personal endings are used with these stems :—

	Singular.		Plural.
1.	-am	1.	-im
2.	-i	2.	-id
3.	- (Past)	3.	-and
	-ad (Pres.)		

(24) From the PAST STEM are formed the Past and Imperfect Tenses.

(i) The *Past Tense* is formed by the addition of the personal endings :—

ḵẖaridam	= *I bought*	ḵẖaridim	= *we bought*
ḵẖaridi	= *you bought*	ḵẖaridid	= *you bought*
ḵẖarid	= *he (she) bought*	ḵẖaridand	= *they bought*

(ii) By prefixing mi- to the Past Tense, the *Imperfect Tense* is formed, e.g. :—

miḵẖaridam = *I was buying*
miḵẖaridi = *you were buying*, etc.

(iii) From the Past Stem is also formed the Past Participle (see para. 29).

(25) From the PRESENT STEM are formed the Imperative, and the Subjunctive, and Present Tenses.

(i) The *Imperative* consists (in the 2nd Person Sing.) of the simple stem, and (in the 2nd Pers. Plur.) of the stem with -id, e.g. :—

<u>kh</u>ar ! = *buy !*   <u>kh</u>arid ! = *buy !* (pl.)

Except, however, in the case of most compound verbs (see Lesson VI), the particle be- (bo- before a syllable with o or u) is prefixed, e.g. :—

be<u>kh</u>ar !   be<u>kh</u>arid !
bokon ! = *do !*   bokonid ! = *do !* (pl.)

but   negâh kon ! = " *look !* " (from negâh kardan)

(ii) The *Subjunctive* is formed by the addition of the Personal Endings to the Present Stem ; as in the Imperative, the prefix be- (bo-) is generally added in the case of simple verbs. It may be used by itself ("let him buy"), or in subordinate sentences ("that he may buy"), etc. (see paras. 44–7).

be<u>kh</u>aram = *let me buy*   be<u>kh</u>arim = *let us buy*
be<u>kh</u>ari   = *may you buy*   be<u>kh</u>arid = *may you buy*
be<u>kh</u>arad = *let him buy*   be<u>kh</u>arand = *let them buy*

(iii) The *Present Tense* is formed by prefixing mi- to the Subjunctive (without be-), e.g. :—

mi<u>kh</u>aram = *I buy*   mi<u>kh</u>arim = *we buy*
mi<u>kh</u>ari   = *you buy*   mi<u>kh</u>arid = *you buy*
mi<u>kh</u>arad = *he (she, it) buys*   mi<u>kh</u>arand = *they buy*

This tense is also frequently used with a Future meaning.

(iv) From the Present Stem are also formed the Present Participles and the Verbal Noun (see para. 29).

(26) The *Negative* of all these tenses is formed by prefixing

the Negative particle na- (accented); be- is then dropped
(but not mi-), e.g. :—

nak͟haridam = *I did not buy*

nak͟har = *do not buy!*

nak͟harad = *let him not buy*

namik͟harim = $\begin{cases} \textit{we do not buy} \\ \textit{we are not buying} \\ \textit{we will not buy} \end{cases}$

N.B.—The verb dâs͟htan "to have" does not take mî-
or be-, even when used by itself; dâram = "I have", etc.
The Subjunctive is expressed by the Perfect Subjunctive—
dâs͟htè bâs͟ham (see para. 34).

(27) In colloquial speech contraction takes place in the
tenses formed from the Present Stem, when that stem ends
in h, v, or a vowel (after which y is normally inserted—
see para. 7); thus from raftan :—

miravam	becomes	miram
miravi	,,	miri
miravad	,,	mirad
miravim	,,	mirim
miravid	,,	mirid
miravand	,,	mirand, etc.

Similarly from âmadan (â)—

beyâyam	becomes	beyâm
beyâyid	,,	beyid, etc.

from k͟hâstan (k͟hâh)—

mik͟hâham becomes mik͟hâm, etc.

from goftan (gu)—

miguyam	becomes	migam
miguyim	,,	migim
miguyand	,,	migand, etc.

Note that these g's
are not palatalized.

from dâdan (deh)—

mideham   becomes midam

midehid   ,,   midid, etc.

Note also that the regular Present Stem of âvardan—âvar—becomes âr, e.g. :—

miyâvaram becomes miyâram

miyâvarid   ,,   miyârid, etc.

Thus the rule may be summarized :—

v, h, and y may be omitted, and in that case—

(i) i absorbs the preceding vowel.

(ii) a absorbs all vowels except â, by which it is itself absorbed.

In certain two-syllable stems, the first vowel is often dropped after be-, mi-, and na- ; e.g. bogzâr (for bogozâr) = " place ! " ; migzâram (for migozâram) = " I will place " (from gozâshtan, stem gozâr).

CONSTRUCTION OF SIMPLE SENTENCES

(28) The regular order of a sentence is—

Subject—Extension of Predicate—Object—Word closely qualifying verb—Verb ;

but this order may be changed for emphasis.

The Object of the Verb may be indicated by placing the particle -râ after it (only, however, when it is definite). The Object may be a single noun, a noun with adjectives, or even a phrase with a Verbal Noun, Infinitive, etc. In all these cases the -râ is placed at the end of the phrase, and not necessarily immediately after the noun.

In colloquial it becomes -o or -â, or very often is omitted altogether.

nôkaram dar mizkhânè   = *my servant prepared supper*
shâm-râ hâzer kard   *in the dining room*
shôfer-e-mâshin-e-ra'is-e-koll = *I saw the driver of the General*
râ dar bâzâr didam   *Manager's car in the bazaar*

When the object is a pronoun, -râ must (in correct speech)
be suffixed to the *separate* forms ; but in colloquial it is more
usual to attach the *pronominal suffixes* direct to the verb,
e.g. didamesh = " I saw him " (instead of ûrâ dîdam).

Many verbs are used with prepositions instead of having
direct objects ; these must be learnt by practice. Some may
have either, e.g. goftamesh or besh goftam = " I said to him " ;
be-manzelam raftam = " I went to my house ", raftam
manzel = " I went home ".

The Plural of the Verb is normally only used for rational
or living beings (see para. 13).

EXERCISE III

(1) dar shahr kasi-râ nadidi ? = **Didn't you see anyone in the
                                    town ?**

(2) balè, âghâ, hassân-e-shôfer- = **Yes, sir, I saw Hassan the
râ didam   driver**

(3) ânjâ chè kâr mikard ?   = **What was he doing there ?**

(4) chè midânam, âghâ ? man   = **How should I know, sir ? I
naporsidam   didn't ask**

(5) besyâr khob ! borô, besh   = **Very well ! go and say to
bogu "har chè zudtar beyâ!"   him " Come as quickly as
                                   possible "**

(6) man tâzè az esfahân   = **I have just come from
âmadam ; dar in shahr   Isfahan ; is there a good
mehmânkhânè-ye-khob hast   hotel in this town ?**
yâ na ?

(7) bale âghâ, dar kheyâbân-e- = Yes, sir, there is a good one
    pahlavi yeki khob hast   in Pahlavi Street

(8) bâ doroshkè borô, ânjâ = Go by droshky, you will
    zudtar mirasid   arrive there sooner

(9) emruz yek guni ârd = To-day I want one sack of
    mikhâham, yek ghuti sabzi   flour, one tin of vegetables
    va yek pâket chây   and one packet of tea

(10) in ârd gerân ast. balè, = This flour is dear. Yes,
    khânom, ghêmatesh zeyâd   madam, its price has
    shod   gone up

(11) mivè-ye-khob dârid ? = Have you some good fruit ?
    balè, khânom, in sibhâ bad   Yes, madam, these apples
    nist, vali an kharbuzehâ   are not bad, but those
    behtarin-e-mivè ast   melons are the best of
                      fruit

(12) khêli khob, yek kharbuzè = Very well, give me one melon
    va yek kilô sib bedeh   and one kilo of apples

PARTICIPLES, AUXILIARIES, IRREGULAR VERBS, ADVERBS

(29) THE following are commonly used :—

Past : formed from the *Past Stem* by the addition of the termination -è, e.g. kardè " done ", raftè " gone ", koshtè " killed ", kharidè " bought ".

Present : (*a*) Agent : formed by adding -andè to the *Present Stem*, e.g. konandè " doing ", " doer ".

(*b*) Action : formed by adding -ân to the Present Stem, e.g. ravân " going ".

When used as nouns, these Particles may take the Plural ending -ân (-gân after -è).

The Past Participle (beside its uses as noun or adjective) is used in the formation of the compound tenses of the verb (see para. 34).

The Present Participles are used both by themselves, e.g. namâyandè = " representative " (from namudan—namâ " to show ") ; and in the formation of compound nouns, e.g. kâr-konandè = " employee ".

The *Gerundive* (expressing future or necessary action) is formed by adding -i to the Infinitive, e.g. raftani = " about to go " ; koshtani = " fit to be killed ".

The *Verbal Noun* (expressing the action of the verb) is formed by adding -esh to the Present Stem, e.g. :—

khâhesh = " wish " (from khâstan—khâh = " to wish ").
kushesh = " effort " (from kushidan—kush = " to try ").

Auxiliaries

(30) The following verbs, besides having their normal meaning, are also used as auxiliaries in the formation of compound tenses :—

budan (bâ<u>sh</u>)   = *to be*
<u>sh</u>odan (<u>sh</u>av) = *to become*
<u>kh</u>âstan (<u>kh</u>âh) = *to wish*

These are conjugated regularly in accordance with the stems given, with the exception of budan which, in addition to a Present Tense formed regularly from bâ<u>sh</u>, has the following :—

Singular.   *Plural.*

1. am   1. im
2. i   2. id } without **mi-**
3. ast, -è   3. and

This form is used with adjectives, and also as the auxiliary.

The meaning of the regular form (mibâ<u>sh</u>am, etc.), is rather indefinite, and almost equals the Subjunctive (may be).

budan also has the following Present Tense, used by itself, and having rather the meaning of " exists, there is " :—

Singular.   *Plural.*

1. hastam   1. hastim
2. hasti   2. hastid
3. hast   3. hastand

(again without mi-)

With na- it becomes nistam, etc., the form also used for the negative of am, i, ast, etc.

Common Irregular Verbs (see para. 22)

(31) âmadan—â   = *come*
âmu<u>kh</u>tan—âmuz   = *learn*

âmi<u>kh</u>tan—âmiz	= *mix*
afzudan—afzâ	= *increase*
andâ<u>kh</u>tan—andâz	= *throw*
bastan—band	= *bind, close, fasten*
bâyestan—bâ	= *ought* (impers.)
bordan—bar	= *carry, take away*
budan—bâ<u>sh</u>	= *be*
dâdan—deh	= *give*
dâ<u>sh</u>tan—dâr	= *have*
dânestan—dân	= *know* (a *thing*—" savoir ")
didan—bin	= *see*
ferestâdan—ferest	= *send*
fereftan—ferib	= *deceive*
farmudan—farmâ	= *command*
foru<u>kh</u>tan—foru<u>sh</u>	= *sell*
goza<u>sh</u>tan—gozar	= *pass by*
gozâ<u>sh</u>tan—gozâr	= *put, place, leave*
ga<u>sh</u>tan (gardidan)—gard	= *become, turn*

(Sometimes used instead of <u>sh</u>odan as **auxiliaries.**)

gereftan—gir	= *take*
goftan—gu	= *say*
istâdan—ist	= *stand*
jostan—ju	= *seek*
kardan—kon	= *do*
kâ<u>sh</u>tan—kâr	= *sow, plant*
<u>kh</u>âstan—<u>kh</u>âh	= *wish*
<u>kh</u>âstan—<u>kh</u>iz	= *rise*
kuftan—kub	= *strike*
mordan—mir	= *die*
ne<u>sh</u>astan—ne<u>sh</u>in	= *sit*
namudan—namâ	= *show*
nave<u>sh</u>tan—navis	= *write*
nehâdan—neh	= *lay down*

oftâdan—oft	= *fall*
po<u>kh</u>tan—paz	= *cook*
paziroftan—pazir	= *accept*
pardâ<u>kh</u>tan—pardâz	= *pay*
raftan—rav	= *go*
ri<u>kh</u>tan—riz	= *pour*
sâ<u>kh</u>tan—sâz	= *make*
sepordan—sepâr	= *entrust*
su<u>kh</u>tan—suz	= *burn*
<u>sh</u>âyestan—<u>sh</u>â	= *be fitting* (impers.)
<u>sh</u>ustan—<u>sh</u>u	= *wash*
(coll. <u>sh</u>ur)	
<u>sh</u>ekastan—<u>sh</u>ekan	= *break*
<u>sh</u>omordan—<u>sh</u>omâr	= *count*
<u>sh</u>enâ<u>kh</u>tan—<u>sh</u>enâs	= *know* (*a person*—"connaître")
<u>sh</u>odan—<u>sh</u>av	= *become*
<u>sh</u>anidan—<u>sh</u>anav	= *hear*
tavânestan—tavân	= *be able*
yâftan—yâb	= *find*
zadan—zan	= *strike*

N.B.—For those interested in the phonetic aspect, it may be noted that the following changes take place.

(i) Modification of stem :—

	Pres. Stem		Past Stem
(*a*)	-â [1]	becomes	-u
(*b*)	-b	,,	-f
(*c*)	-nd	,,	-s
	-rd	,,	-<u>sh</u>
(*d*)	-h	,,	-s

[1] = regular formation also found.

	Pres. Stem		Past Stem
(e)	-n [1]	becomes	-s [2]
	-in	,,	-i
(f)	-r [1]	,,	-r [2]
	-r	,,	-sh
(g)	-s [1]	,,	-sh [2]
	-s	,,	-kh
(h)	-sh [1]	,,	-kh
(i)	-v	,,	-f
	-av	,,	-u

N.B.—shav = shodan ;   (bov) = budan.

	(j) -z	becomes	-kh [2]

(ii) Besides the regular ending -idan, the following may be used after consonants or vowels :—

-âdan, -estan, -(o, e)ftan,[2]

the last two often with contraction after a vowel.

(iii) The following verbs have different stems for Present and Past :—

bin —did	bâsh—bud
â —âmad	deh —dâd
khiz—khâst	kon —kard
zan —zad	

ADVERBS

(32) Many nouns of time, place, and manner (with or without qualifying adjective or noun) may be used as adverbs without change, e.g. :—

ruz(i)	= by day
ruz-e-ta'til	= holiday
shab	= at night
sobh	= in the morning, to-morrow

---

[1] See Note [1], p. 33.   [2] = vowel change may also take place.

fardâ sobh	= *to-morrow morning*
fardâ sobh zud	= *early to-morrow morning*
zohr	= *at noon*
asr	= *late afternoon*

mâh ⎫
haftè ⎬ -e-âyandè = *next* ⎰ *month*
sâl ⎭ -e-goza<u>sh</u>tè = *last* ⎨ *week*
                                        ⎩ *year*

yek daf'è	= *once*
taraf-e-râst, <u>ch</u>ap ⎫	
dast-e-râst, <u>ch</u>ap ⎭	= *on (to) the right, left*
injâ	= *here*
anjâ	= *there*
harjâ, hamè jâ	= *everywhere*
intôr, ântôr ⎫	
injur(è), ânjur(è) ⎬	= *thus, in this (that) way*
ingunè, ângunè ⎭	

Most adjectives may be used as adverbs without change,
e.g. :—

râst ⎫
sahih ⎬ = *right, true*
dorost ⎭

râst	= *straight (ahead)*
zud	= *quick*
dir	= *late*
digar	= *other, more*
<u>kh</u>êli	= *much, many*
zeyâd	= *too much*

(33) Other adverbs proper, besides those given in the list
of prepositions (para. 19), are as follows :—

                            (a) *Time*

emruz	= *to-day*	fardâ	= *to-morrow*
diruz	= *yesterday*	di<u>sh</u>ab	= *last night*

pasfardâ	= *the day after to-morrow*	pariruz	= *the day before yesterday*
hami<u>sh</u>è	= *always*	hi<u>ch</u>va<u>gh</u>t, har<u>ge</u>z	= *never*
hâlâ	= *now*	al'ân	= *presently*
mâheyânè	= *monthly*	sâleyânè	= *yearly*
pârsâl	= *last year*	emsâl	= *this year*
hanuz	= *still*	hanuz . . . . . na	= *not yet*
konun	= *at present*	tâ konun	= *up to now*

N.B.—<u>ch</u>and ruz pi<u>sh</u> (<u>gh</u>abl) = *some days ago*

<u>ch</u>and ruz ba'd = *some days after*

(**tâ**) <u>ch</u>and ruz digar = *for a few days more, in a few days*

(b) Manner, etc.

hamrâh	= *together* (also as preposition)	âhestè, âstè yavâ<u>sh</u>	⎫⎬⎭ = *slowly*
bâ-ham	= *together* (*united*)		
tanhâ	= *alone*	hi<u>ch</u> hi<u>ch</u>i	⎫⎬ . . . . na = *not at all*
bas	= *enough*	niz	⎫
ham	= *even*	ham	⎬ = *also*
pas	= ⎰ *then* ⎱ *in that case*	albattè	= *certainly*

Many Arabic adverbs (generally ending in -an) are used in Persian ; a few common ones are :—

a<u>gh</u>allan	= *at least*	<u>gh</u>âleban	= *generally*
tab'an	= *naturally*	ta<u>gh</u>riban	= *nearly*
sâbe<u>gh</u>an	= *formerly*	a<u>kh</u>iran	= *lately*
movagh<u>gh</u>atan	= *temporarily*	fe'lan	= *actually*

aslan	= *originally*	ba'd-ez-zohr	= *in the afternoon*
belhag̲h̲ig̲h̲è	= *in truth, fact*	belâk̲h̲erè	= *at last*

EXERCISE IV

(1) sâl-e-goza_sh_tè kojâ manzel dâ_sh_tid ? = **Where did you live during the past year ?**

(2) tâ hâlâ dar esfahân mândam, vali yek mâh pi_sh_ be-tehrân âmadam = **Until now I stayed in Isfahan, but one month ago I came to Tehran**

(3) o _ch_and vag̲h̲t digar injâ mimânid ? = **And how long will you stay here ?**

(4) yek manzel-e-tâzè k̲h̲ari- dam ; yek sâl bi_sh_tar mimâ- nam = **I have bought a new house ; I will stay here a year or more**

(5) in kâr _ch_erâ zudtar hâzer na_sh_od ? = **Why has this work not been finished sooner ?**

(6) âg̲h̲â, tâ diruz fag̲h̲at yek nafar budam, vali emruz yek rafig̲h̲i mâl-e-man âmad = **Till yesterday, sir, I was by myself, but to-day a companion of mine came**

(7) k̲h̲êli k̲h̲ob, bâ_sh_ad ; lâken hâlâ ku_sh_e_sh_ bokon = **Very well, that may be ; but now make an effort**

(8) yek farrâ_sh_i injâ beferest ; kâr-e-fôri dâram = **Send a messenger here ; I have some urgent work**

(9) dar hâl, âg̲h̲â, farrâ_sh_i hi_ch_ nadârim = **At the moment, sir, we have no messenger**

(10) kê hâzer mi_sh_avad ? = **When will he be ready ?**

(11) namidânam, âg̲h̲â, vali har _ch_è zudtar miferestam = **I don't know, sir, but I will send him as soon as possible**

(12) ânjâ ben_sh_inid âg̲h̲â ; hâlâ begid—dar râh _ch_è _ch_iz didid ? = **Sit down there ; now tell me, what did you see on the road ?**

(13) âghâ, dar posht-e-mâshin = Sir, I was asleep in the back
    khâbidam ; chizi nadidam   of the car ; I saw nothing

(14) hamishè dorugh migid ; = You always tell lies ; the
    râh kheli gôd dârad—chè tôr   road has many holes—
    khâbidid ?   how could you sleep ?

Lesson V

AUXILIARIES, IMPERSONAL AND CAUSATIVE VERBS, SUMMARY OF TENSES

(34) THE Auxiliaries mentioned in the last lesson are used with parts of the verb to form the compound tenses.

(i) "*budan*" is used after the Past Participle to form the various tenses of the *Perfect* (of both transitive and intransitive verbs).

Perfect : kardè am = *I have done.*

Pluperfect : kardè budam = *I had done.*

Perfect Subjunctive : kardè bâsham = *I may, would have done.*

(ii) "*khâstan*" (in the Present Tense without mi-) is used *before* the Past Stem to express the *Future* (when it is necessary to make it definite ; normally the Present Tense may be used with Future meaning).

khâham kard = I will do

(iii) "*shodan*" is used in all its tenses with the Past Participle to form the *Passive.*

koshtè shod	= *he was killed*
koshtè mishod	= *he was being killed*
koshtè shô	= *be killed !*
koshtè shavad	= *let him be killed*
koshtè mishavad	= *he is being killed*
koshtè shodè ast	= *he has been killed*
koshtè shodè bud	= *he had been killed*
koshtè shodè bâshad	= *he will (may) have been killed*
koshtè khâhad shod	= *he will be killed*

N.B.—(*a*) " budan " *never* has a Passive meaning.
(*b*) The negative particle " na- " is prefixed to :—

(i) The Past Participle, e.g. :—

nakardè am = *I have not done*

(ii) k͟hâstan, e.g. :—

nak͟hâham kard = *I will not do*

(iii) the relevant part of " s͟hodan " (in accordance with (i) and (ii)).

kos͟htè nas͟hod = *he was not killed*
kos͟htè nas͟hodè ast = *he has not been killed*
kos͟htè nak͟hâhad s͟hod = *he will not be killed*

(*c*) " k͟hâstan " is, of course, also used in its ordinary meaning of " to wish ". In this case the Present is conjugated regularly with mi-, and it also has all the other tenses of the verb (it may thus be found compounded with itself, e.g.—

k͟hâham k͟hâst = *I will wish*).

With this meaning it is followed by the Subjunctive (see para. 44), and may also have the meaning of " to be about to ", e.g. :—

k͟hâstam beravam = $\begin{cases} I \text{ wished to go} \\ I \text{ was about to go} \end{cases}$

(*d*) In colloquial the use of the Perfect is very common, and frequently the auxiliary is dropped if the meaning is clear without it.

(*e*) " gas͟htan " and " gardidan " are sometimes used instead of " s͟hodan " in the Passive. All three may, of course, be used in their ordinary meaning of " to become ", with all the various tenses.

IMPERSONAL VERBS

(35) (i) The impersonal Verb " bâyestan " (root " bâ ")
is used only in the 3rd Person Singular of the Past and
Present Tenses (without mi-) to express " ought, must ".

(a) When the Subject is expressed, it is placed (sometimes
followed by -râ) in front of bâyestan, which is followed by
the verb in the Subjunctive.

hasan bâyad (bâd) nân beyârad = *Hasan must bring some bread*

tô (râ) bâd $\Big\}$ hâzer bâ<u>sh</u>i   = *you must be ready*
bâdat

The Past Tense (which is less common) must be followed
by the Perfect Subjunctive, e.g. :—

<u>sh</u>omâ bâyest zudtar âmadè = *you ought to have come more*
    bâ<u>sh</u>id   *quickly*

(b) But when the subject is not expressed, or is indefinite
(that is, when the obligation is general), " bâyestan " is
followed by the Past Stem, e.g. :—

harkas bâyad esfahân raft = *everyone ought to go to Isfahan*

N.B.—The use of the Past Stem does not mean that the
meaning is past.

(ii) " <u>sh</u>âyestan " (root " <u>sh</u>â ") is rarely used except in
the 3rd Person Singular of the Present Tense—<u>sh</u>âyad (<u>sh</u>âd)—
in which form it has become little more than an adverb
meaning " perhaps " ; it does not affect the construction of
the sentence.

(iii) " tavânestan " (root " tavân ") = " to be able "—is
used personally when the subject is expressed, and is then
followed by the Subjunctive :—

namitavânam (namitunam) fârsi = *I cannot read Persian*
    bekhânam

When, however, the meaning is general (as with " bâyestan " above), it is used impersonally with the Past Stem ; in such cases it usually does not have the Personal ending :—

in kâr-râ (hi<u>ch</u>kas) namitavân = *one cannot (no one can) do*
kard   *this work*

N.B.—The usual contraction of -tavân- is -tun-.

Causative Verbs

(36) These are generally formed by the addition of -ân to the Present Stem, the Infinitive ending being either -dan or -idan, e.g. :—

rasidan = to arrive
rasân(i)dan = to bring (to make to arrive).

Sometimes there is contraction, e.g. :—

raftan (rav) = to go
rândan (for ravândan) = to drive (to make to go).

Occasionally the Causative sense is given by lengthening the vowel of the stem, e.g. :—

gozâ<u>sh</u>tan = *to place* from goza<u>sh</u>tan = *to pass*.

Summary of Tenses

(37) *Past* : completed action in the past ; raft = " he went " ; sometimes also in the present or future, e.g. hâlâ raft = " he has just gone " ; hâzer <u>sh</u>od = " it is ready " ; harkojâ raft = " wherever he goes ".

Imperfect : continuous action in the past ; miraft = " he was going, he used to go ".

Imperative : command ; borô = " go ! "

Subjunctive : (*a*) by itself, in a jussive sense ; beravad = " let him go ".

(*b*) In various subordinate sentences (of which two examples have been given above—see paras. 34, 35, 44–7).

Present : generally in a continuous sense ; miravad = " he is going, he goes " ; but also in a future sense : " he will go."

Perfect : action which, or the effect of which, is still continuing ; raftè ast = " he has gone " (as opposed to " he went ").

Pluperfect : the Perfect in a past time-reference ; raftè bud = " he had gone ".

Perfect Subjunctive : past action in subordinate clauses where the Subjunctive is required.

Future : a definitely future action ; khâhad raft = " he will go ".

OTHER PARTS OF THE VERB

Infinitive : generally used as a noun " the act of . . . ") ; âb-e-khordan = " drinking water " ; khordan-e-âb = " the drinking of water ".

Participles : Past—one } used as adjective, adverb, or
          Present—two } noun.

Gerundive : necessary, suitable, or future action ; " about to, fit to, etc."

Verbal Noun : the action of the verb in the abstract.

N.B.—The object of an Infinitive or a Verbal Noun follows it, and is linked to it by the Ezâfè.

EXERCISE V

(1) fardâ sobh zud be-tehrân = **To-morrow I will go to** khâham raft   **Tehran**

(2) besyâr <u>kh</u>ob, â<u>gh</u>â ; bâ = Very well, sir ; by which
kodâm râh mi<u>kh</u>âhid road do you wish to go ?
beravid ?

(3) râh-e-<u>gh</u>om berim ; az = Let us go by the Qum road ;
râh-e-kâ<u>sh</u>ân sâftar ast it is smoother than the
Kashan road

(4) dar <u>gh</u>om masjed-e- = In Qum you will see their
<u>gh</u>a<u>sh</u>ang-e-ânjâ <u>kh</u>âhid did beautiful mosque

(5) masjed-e-<u>gh</u>om <u>gh</u>a<u>sh</u>ang- = The Qum mosque is beautiful
è, ammâ amârathâ-ye-tâzè- but the new buildings of
ye-tehrân behtar-è Tehran are better

(6) râst migid ; vali <u>kh</u>ârejihâ = You are right ; but foreign-
amârathâ-ye-kohnè hami<u>sh</u>è ers always see the old
mibinand buildings

(7) bogu rezâ, " <u>sh</u>âm-râ = Tell Reza to get supper
zudtar hâzer bokon " ; ready earlier ; is it
mi<u>sh</u>ad ya nami<u>sh</u>ad ? possible ?

(8) <u>sh</u>âyad momken ast, â<u>gh</u>â ; = Perhaps it is possible, sir ;
lâken emruz <u>kh</u>êli kâr dârad but he has a lot of work
to-day

(9) êb nist ; bâyad har <u>ch</u>è = Never mind ; he must get
zudtar hâzer konad it ready as soon as
possible

(10) bâ in râh mitavân raft ? = Can one go by this road ?

(11) bâ lâri <u>sh</u>âyad momken-è ; = By lorry it may be possible ;
vali bâ mâ<u>sh</u>in-e-<u>sh</u>omâ but you cannot go in your
namitavânid beravid car

(12) hâlâ <u>ch</u>and sâl dar irân = I have been driving in Iran
mâ<u>sh</u>in mirândam, mesl-e-in for several years, and I
râh hargez nadidè am have never seen a road
like this

(13) diruz kojâ raftè budid ? = Where had you gone
injâ <u>kh</u>edmat - e - <u>sh</u>omâ yesterday ? I came here

âmadè am, nôkaratân goft "birun raftè" — to call on you, and your servant said you had gone out

(14) mota'assef am; yek khordè nâkhosh budam, az sabab-e-khordan-e-gusht-e-kharâb = I am sorry ; I was rather ill, through eating bad meat

(15) ânhâ che kâr mikonand ? = What are those people doing ?

(16) bar-e-forukh tan-e-asbâ-beshân âmadè and = They have come to sell their goods

COMPOUND VERBS, CONJUNCTIONS

(38) ONE of the most characteristic features of Persian is its use of compound verbs, that is to say, verbs which are formed by using a noun, verbal noun, adverb, adjective, preposition, etc., with a common verb having some such meaning as " to do, make, become ", etc. Some of these have straightforward meanings, but many have idiomatic uses, and these are among the commonest in ordinary speech.

Examples

(39) *Verbs compounded with prepositions or adverbs :—*

bâz didan	= *to inspect*
kardan	= *to open*
goftan	= *to repeat*
âmadan	= *to come back*
bar dâshtan	= *to pick up*
gashtan	= *to return*
khâstan (khiz)	= *to rise*
birun kardan	= *to throw out, drive out, dismiss*
dar kashidan	= *to draw in*
âmadan	= *to come in* (dar), *out* (az)
âvardan	= *to bring in* (dar), *out* (az)
gereftan	= *to break out* (war)
forud âmadan	= *to land* (plane)
pâ'in kardan	= *to lower*
pish âmadan	= *to come forward, happen*
vâ istâdan	= *to wait*
dâshtan	= *to appoint*

46

(40) *Verbs compounded with adjectives.*

tang	kardan	= *tighten*
shol	,,	= *loosen*
boland	,,	= *raise, erect*
kharâb	,,	= *spoil, damage*
bidâr	,,	= *waken*
lokht	,,	= *strip*
lâzem	dâshtan	= *require*
dorugh	goftan	= *lie*
râst	,,	= *tell the truth*
kharâb	shodan	= *be spoilt*
moltafet	,,	= *understand* (polite)
sevâr	,,	= *be mounted*

(41) *Verbs compounded with a noun,* especially a verbal noun. This is the most usual way of forming a verb from an Arabic noun. Often the noun is preceded by a preposition.

farâmush	kardan	= *forget*
pêdâ	,,	= *find*
negâh	,,	= *look at, watch*
kushesh	,,	= *exert one's self, try*
sabr	,,	= *wait*
vel	,,	= *let go, put down*
tâ	,,	= *fold up*
yâd	âvardan	= *remember, call to mind*
gir	âmadan	= *be available, procurable*
gamân	bordan	= *imagine, suppose*
neshân	dâdan	= *show*
fohsh	,,	= *abuse*
ejâzè	,,	= *allow*
negâh	dâshtan	= *stop*
hâl	,,	= *be in good health*
dust	,,	= *love*

yâd	gereftan	= *learn*
zahmat	ka<u>sh</u>idan	= *take trouble*
sigâri	,,	= *smoke a cigarette*
tul	,,	= *last, take time*
tasvir	,,	= *draw (a picture)*
sarmâ	<u>kh</u>ordan	= *catch cold*
za<u>kh</u>m	,,	= *be wounded, bruised*
zamin	,,	= *hit, fall on, the ground*
<u>kh</u>âb	raftan	= *go to sleep*
az yâd	,,	= *forget*
eltefât	namudan	= *show kindness, pay attention*
joft	<u>sh</u>odan	= *be joined, united (of two)*
harf	zadan	= *speak*
âte<u>sh</u>	,,	= *light (fire)*

The following points are to be noticed :—

(i) The prefixes mi-, be-, and na-, and the auxiliary <u>kh</u>âstan are inserted between the verb and its compounded word, e.g. ku<u>sh</u>e<u>sh</u> mikonam = " I am exerting myself ".   be-, however, is very often omitted, especially in subordinate sentences, and always after the preposition " bar ", e.g. bar <u>kh</u>iz = " rise ".   In this and in a few other cases, in which the preposition has become very closely linked with the verb, " <u>kh</u>âstan " is placed before it, e.g. <u>kh</u>âhad bar <u>kh</u>âst = " he shall rise ".

(ii) These verbs are treated for grammatical purposes just as though they were simple verbs, that is to say, if they are transitive the direct object may take the suffix -râ, and so on.   If a pronominal suffix is used (in colloquial) it is suffixed to the compounded word, e.g. birune<u>sh</u> kon = " throw it out ", tâ<u>sh</u> kon = " fold it up ".

(iii) Groups (*b*) and (*c*) are especially used when in English we use causative verbs, e.g. " to loosen ", " waken ", etc.

(iv) kardan is by far the commonest of these verbs, and in colloquial is often used when the correct verb would be one of the others.

Conjunctions.—(For those used with Subordinate Sentences see paras. 43–52.)

(42)

va, o	= *and*
ham	= *also, and*
ham . . . . . . (va) ham	= *both . . . . . and*
yâ, va yâ	= *or*
yâ . . . . . . yâ	= *either . . . . or*
ammâ } lâken }	= *but*
vali } na . . . . va na }	= *neither . . . . . nor*

EXERCISE VI

(1) fârsi balad-id, âghâ ? = **Do you know Persian ?**

(2) balè, âghâ, kami yâd gereftam, vali khob harf namizanam = **Yes, I have learnt a little, but I do not speak it well**

(3) êb nadârad, dar chand mâh digar khob âmukhtè bâshid = **Never mind, in a few months you will have learnt it well**

(4) injâ sabr konid ; chand daghighè digar bar migardam = **Wait here ; I shall be back in a few minutes**

(5) âghâ, injâ sard ast ; shâyad sarmâ mikhoram = **It is cold here, sir ; I may catch cold**

(6) khêli khob, dâkhel-e-châykhânè vâ ist ; ânjâ garm ast = **Very well, wait in the tea-shop ; it is warm there**

(7) âghâ-ye-doktor, saram khêli dard mikonad ; yek khordè davâ lâzem dâram = **Doctor, my head aches badly ; I need some medicine**

(8) in habbè-râ bo<u>kh</u>or, hâlat= **Take this pill, you will soon**
    zud behtar mi<u>sh</u>ad   **be better**

(9) mâ <u>kh</u>êli tond nayâmadim? = **Have we not come quickly ?**
    diruz harakat kardim, emruz   **We left yesterday, and**
    rasidè im   **arrived to-day**

(10) bâ mâ<u>sh</u>in safar kardè id = **Have you travelled by road**
    yâ bâ râh-e-âhan ?   **or by train ?**

(11) bâ râh-e-âhan âmadim ; = **We came by train ; it is not**
    gerân nist, va az mâ<u>sh</u>in   **expensive, and it is much**
    <u>kh</u>êli zudtar miravad   **quicker than by car**

(12) mitavânid pelâo dorost = **Can you make pilau ? I am**
    bokonid ;   pelâo-e-irâni   **very fond of Iranian pilau**
    <u>kh</u>eli dust dâram

(13) balè, â<u>gh</u>â, balad am ; = **Yes, sir, I can ; I can also**
    ham   mitunam   kabâb   **cook kabobs. Would you**
    bepazam. mêl dârid ?   **like some ?**

(14) <u>sh</u>omâ pi<u>sh</u> az in kojâ kâr = **Before this where did you**
    mikardid ?   **work ?**

(15) dar kâr<u>kh</u>ânè-ye-in   = **I was a fitter in the work-**
    <u>sh</u>erkat mikânik budam   **shop of this company**

(16) <u>ch</u>erâ e<u>kh</u>râj <u>sh</u>odid ?   = **Why were you discharged ?**

(17) <u>kh</u>odam este'fâ kardam, = **I resigned and went home**
    raftam velâyat

SUBORDINATE SENTENCES

INDIRECT STATEMENTS, QUESTIONS, ETC.

(43) THE particle kè " that " is generally inserted after the main verb, the statement or question following in its original form, e.g. :—

goft kè nâshtâ hâzer ast = *he said that breakfast was ready*

porsid kè nâshtâ hâzer ast yâ na = *he asked if breakfast was ready*

azesh porsid kè râh-e-esfahân= *he asked where the road to* kojâ-st *Isfahan was*

WISHES AND COMMANDS

(44) The subordinate verb is placed in the Subjunctive, the clause often being introduced by kè.

mikhâham bevelâyatam bera- = *I want to go to my native* vam (correct), mikhâm *place* beram velâyat (colloquial)

besh amr farmud (kè) sabr = *he ordered him to wait* konad

CONSECUTIVE CLAUSES

(45) These clauses are introduced by inserting some such expression as inghadr = " this amount ", ântôr= " that manner ", in the main clause, followed by kè with the Present or Past (for definite consequences) or Subjunctive (for indefinite consequences).

intôr s̱ẖekâyat kard kè ek̲ẖrâj = *he complained so much that*
   s̱ẖod   *he was discharged*
in tanâb âng̲ẖadr mohkam nist = *this rope is not strong enough*
   kè in bâr bekas̱ẖad   *to pull this load*

FINAL (PURPOSE) CLAUSES

(46) The Subjunctive, usually introduced by tâ = " so
that ", " in order that " ; (kè may also be used, or the conjunction may be omitted altogether).

bâ mâs̱ẖin safar kard tâ zudtar = *he travelled by car in order*
   berasad   *to arrive sooner*
raftam   manzel   kolâham = *I went home to get my hat*
   begiram

RESULT

(47) tâ also indicates the result of an action, with the meaning " until ", " with the result that ", in which case it
takes the Past tense (even when in English we use the
Present or Future).

bâ mâs̱ẖin safar kard tâ be- = *he travelled by car until he*
   esfahân rasid   *reached Isfahan*
kus̱ẖes̱ẖ kard tâ kâres̱ẖ sar-e- = *he exerted himself so that his*
   vag̲ẖt k̲ẖalâs bud   *work was ready in time*
injâ vâ ist tâ bar gas̱ẖtam   = *wait here till I come back*

RELATIVE CLAUSES

(48) (i) The only true relative clauses are those in which the
antecedent is one of the demonstrative or indefinite pronouns in, ân, etc. These are followed by the pronoun c̱ẖè
= " which ".

ânchè migid râst-è	= *what you say is true*
harchè bâshad	= *whatever (however) it may be*
chonânchè farmudid, havâ-ye- emrûz hich khob nist	= *as you said, the weather to-day is not at all good*
bâ vojud-e-ânchè besh goftand, tasmim kard tanhâ safar bokonad	= *in spite of what they said to him, he decided to travel alone*

(ii) However, most Relative Clauses consist of a complete sentence placed in apposition to the main sentence. The connection is shown by having in it a pronoun or pronominal suffix linking back to the antecedent in the main sentence (though this pronoun may be omitted when it is the direct subject or object of the subordinate verb).

When the antecedent is a definite noun, it takes the suffix -i (unaccented), and the conjunction kè is placed before the subordinate clause ; but if the antecedent is indefinite, both these are omitted.

The following examples illustrate the various usages :—

chand nafar kârger didam | râh-râ ta'mir mikardand	= *I saw some workmen (who were) repairing the road*
yek shôfer didam | mâshinesh dar râh kharâb shodè bud	= *I saw a driver whose car had broken down on the road*
asbâbhâ-i-râ | kè | kharid-am(esh) | be-kârkhânè fere-stâdam	= *I sent the tools which I bought to the workshop*
farrâshi | kè | kághez-râ besh dâdam | kojâ raft ?	= *where has the office boy gone to whom I gave the letter ?*

After the Personal Pronouns -i is omitted, but kè is retained.

shomâ kè hâzer budid hâdesè- râ nadidid ?	= *did not you who were present see the accident ?*

N.B.—kè does not mean "who" or "which", but "that"; the above sentences therefore read literally :—

..... workmen | they were .....
..... a driver | his car had .....
..... the tools | that | I bought them .....
..... the office boy | that | I gave ..... to him .....
.....you | that | you were present .....

(49) This Relative construction has many extended uses, which the following examples illustrate :—

vaghti kè âmadid birun budam	= *when you came I was outside*
ânjâ-i kè raftid <u>h</u>ich kasi nadidid ?	= *(there) where you went, did you see no one ?*
Cf. dar mô<u>gh</u>e'i kè	= *at the moment when ....*
ruzi kè	= *on the day when ......*
az ruzi kè injâ âmadam, tâ hâlâ <u>h</u>ich <u>kh</u>ari nadidam	= *since (from the day that) I came here (till now), I have not seen a donkey*
har va<u>gh</u>t kârat <u>kh</u>alâs <u>sh</u>odè (ast), manzel borô	= *when(ever) (as soon as) your work is finished, go home*
har jâ (har kojâ) mirid, chizhâ-ye-<u>gh</u>arib mibinid	= *wherever you go, you (will) see strange things*

An important use is the construction of a subordinate sentence introduced by a preposition or prepositional phrase; the latter is followed by in or ân with kè (= "the fact that"), e.g. :—

bâ in kè havâ <u>kh</u>ob nist, fardâ mi<u>kh</u>âm harakat bokonam	= *although (in spite of the fact that) the weather is not good, I wish to leave to-morrow*
ba'd az ân kè raftè ast, nazmiyè âmadè ast	= *after he had gone the police came*

az sabab-e-ân kè mohemmât = *because of (the fact that) the*
    vâred   na<u>sh</u>odè,   sarbâzhâ   *ammunition had not arrived,*
    taslim <u>sh</u>odand   *the soldiers surrendered*

The following (and similar) uses of kè are closely related to the above :—

hâlâ kè be-tehrân rasidim, yek = *now that we have arrived at*
    mehmân<u>kh</u>ânè pêdâ konid   *Tehran, find a hotel*
ba'd, kè raftè bud, pâltô<u>sh</u> = *afterwards, when he had gone,*
    pêdâ <u>sh</u>odè bud   *his overcoat was found*
hâlâ <u>ch</u>and ruz ast (kè) post = *the post has not come for*
    na-y-âmadè ast   *several days*

CAUSAL CLAUSES

(50) In addition to the Relative construction (as exemplified above), the following special causal conjunctions are used :—
<u>zi</u>râ(kè), <u>ch</u>un(kè), both with similar meanings.

N.B.—<u>ch</u>un (without kè) also means when.

zirâ-kè <u>sh</u>ôferam na<u>kh</u>o<u>sh</u> bud, = *because my driver was ill,*
    <u>kh</u>odam mâ<u>sh</u>in-râ mirândam   *I was driving the car myself*
<u>ch</u>un-kè mi<u>kh</u>âstam <u>sh</u>ahr = *because I wanted to go to*
    beram, <u>sh</u>o<u>gh</u>lam <u>kh</u>alâs   *the town, I did not finish*
    nakardam   *my work*

CONDITIONAL SENTENCES

(51) The Conditional particle is agar, ar " if ".

The different constructions are best shown by the following examples ; it will be seen that the Past, Perfect, or Pluperfect is generally used in the Protasis (the " if " clause), even when it is future in meaning.

Future

agar ânjâ raftid, pedaram = *if you go there, you will see*
    <u>kh</u>âhid did   *my father*

agar ânjâ raftid, pedaram = *if you were to go there, you*
    didid   *would see my father*

Present

agar hâzer $\begin{cases} \text{id} \\ \text{shodid, pas berim} \end{cases}$ = *if you are ready, then let us go*

agar pul dâshtam, lebâs-e-tâzè = *if I had some money, I would*
    mikharidam   *buy some new clothes*

Past

agar mâshin-râ dorost kardè = *if he has repaired the car,*
    ast, pas momken ast harakat   *then we can start*
    konim

agar intôr eshtebâh nakardè = *if he had not made this*
    bud, in hâdesè vâghe' nashodè   *mistake, this accident would*
    bud   *not have happened*

(52) *Concessive Clauses* are constructed similarly, the
conjunction being agarchè " although ". The main clause
usually begins with ammâ " but ".

agarchè sarbâzhâ khastè bu- = *although the soldiers were*
    dand, ammâ tavaghghof   *tired, they did not halt*
    nakardand

" if not " is expressed by agarna or va ellâ (Ar.),
the following main clause being generally introduced by
" pas ".

EXERCISE VII

(1) borô bogu hasan-e-shôfer = **Go and tell Hasan the driver**
    mâshinesh zud injâ beyârad   **to bring his car here**
                                 quickly

(2) âghâ, mêl dârid beshahr = **Do you wish to go to the**
    beravid ?   **town, sir ?**

(3) balè, mikhâm chand asbâb- = Yes, I want to buy a few
e-lâzemè bekharam   necessary articles

(4) ejâzè   midehid,   man = Will you permit me to come
hamrâhatân beyâyam ?   with you ?

(5) befarmâ-id, âghâ ;   = Please do, sir ; sit beside me
pahluyam benshin

(6) emruz mikhâham be-shahr- = To-day I wish to go to the
e-esfahân beravam, chunkè   town of Isfahan, because
masâjedesh hanuz nadidè am   I have not yet seen its
                         mosques

(7) agar kârgerân sar-e-vaght = If the workmen do not come
nayâmadè and, ânhâ bâyad   in time, they must be
ekhrâj beshavand   discharged

(8) bâshad, âghâ, vali khâhesh = Very well, sir, but I request
mikonam yek forsat digar   you to give them one more
beshân bedehid   chance

(9) kâghez-hâ-i-râ   kè   emruz = I will take the letters which
sobh vâred shodand mibaram   came this morning

(10) dar khosus-e-ân bâ ra'is- = I have to see the head of the
e-edârè kâr dâram   department in connection
                         with them

(11) vaghtikè   kârat   khalâs = When your work is finished,
shod, be-man khabar bedeh   tell me

(12) ghabl az ân kè sar-e-kâr = Before you go to work, come
raftid, pish-e-man beyâyid   and see me

(13) omid   ast   fardâ   havâ = I hope the weather will be
behtar shod ; ghâleban dar   better to-morrow ; it is
behâr mesl-e-in nist   not usually like this in
                         spring

(14) agar fekr kardam kè intor = If I had known that it would
bâshad,   hichvaght   injâ   be like this, I would never
nayâmadam   have come here

NUMERALS

(53) THE Cardinal Numerals are as follows :—

yek, yey	= *one*
dô	= *two*
sè	= *three*
chahâr, châr	= *four*
panj	= *five*
shesh	= *six*
haft	= *seven*
hasht	= *eight*
noh	= *nine*
dah	= *ten*
yâzdah, -deh	= *eleven*
davâzdah, -deh	= *twelve*
sizdah, -deh sinzdah, -deh	} = *thirteen*
chahârdah, -deh chârdah, -deh	} = *fourteen*
pânzdah, -deh	= *fifteen*
shânzdah, -deh	= *sixteen*
hevdah, -deh	= *seventeen*
hijdah, -deh hizhdah, -deh hezhdah, -deh	} = *eighteen*
nuzdah, -deh	= *nineteen*
bist	= *twenty*
bist-o-yek	= *twenty-one*

bist-o-dô	= *twenty-two*
etc.	*etc.*
si	= *thirty*
chehel	= *forty*
panjâh	= *fifty*
shast	= *sixty*
haftâd	= *seventy*
hashtâd	= *eighty*
navad	= *ninety*
sad	= *hundred*
yeksad	= *one hundred*
davist	= *two hundred*
sisad	= *three hundred*
chahârsad / chârsad	= *four hundred*
pânsad	= *five hundred*
sheshsad	= *six hundred*
haftsad	= *seven hundred*
hashtsad	= *eight hundred*
nohsad	= *nine hundred*
hazâr	= *thousand*
yek hazâr	= *one thousand*
dô hazâr	= *two thousand*
etc.	*etc.*
melyun	= *million*

(54) (*a*) Certain peculiarities must be noticed :—

The alternative pronunciations in the " tens ".

The change that takes place when the units are combined with -dah and -sad, especially the spelling sisad for " three hundred " (not to be taken for " thirty hundred ", which of course would be sè hazâr).

The various alternative forms, which are very common in colloquial.

(b) The Cardinals are not inflected, though when they are used as nouns—

yek may take the indefinite ending -i : yeki (in colloquial often even when qualifying a noun).

sad, hazâr may take the plural endings -hâ and -ân.

(c) Compound Numerals are formed by linking them together with the conjunction o " and ", the largest numeral coming first, e.g. :—

$$1940 = \text{hazâr o nohsad o chehel}$$
$$37{,}288 = \text{si o haft hazâr o davist o hashtâd o hasht}$$

(d) The Cardinals are followed by the noun in the Singular, without change.

sè ketâb　　　　= *three books*
chehel tofang　= *forty guns*

(55) Frequently a noun is inserted after the numeral (with some such meaning as " unit ", " individual ", etc.). In colloquial the usual one is tâ " fold ", " unit ", which has become so closely linked to the numeral as to be part of it, even when there is no following noun (it is also used with chand, when it means " how many "); e.g. châr tâ bil = " four spades " ; chand tâ guni dârid ?—sinzdah tâ = " how many sacks have you ?—thirteen ". tâ is not used after yek, the form yeki being used instead.

This use of tâ with a noun is not considered very elegant, and should be avoided when speaking with educated people, especially when the numeral refers to persons. For the latter nafar " person " may be used : yek nafar amniyè = " an ' amniyè ' guard (country police) " ; panj nafar sarbâz = " five soldiers ". Other similar nouns are also found, but they are survivals from an older, more florid style, and their use in general is discouraged in modern correct speech.

N.B.—The Ezâfè is not inserted after these nouns (nor generally after a noun inserted between a numeral and another noun, e.g. yek s͟his͟hè âb = " a glass of water ") ; they are regarded as indefinite (see paras. 10, 11).

ORDINAL NUMERALS

(56) The Ordinals are formed by adding the suffix -om to the end of the Cardinal, whether this be a simple or a compound numeral ; e.g. c͟hahârom = " fourth " ; bist-o-nohom = " twenty-ninth ". The following forms, however, must be carefully noted :—

first = avval (Arabic ; the regular form is used, however, when it occurs in a compound numeral, e.g. si-o-yekom = " thirty-first ").

second = dovvom
third = sevvom
thirtieth = siyom

avval is often used as an adverb with the meaning " first, firstly ". The others are not used thus, their place being taken by the Arabic forms, of which the following are worthy of note :—

sâneyan = *secondly*
sâlesan = *thirdly*

FRACTIONS

(57) The Persian forms of the fractions are rarely used (they are formed by adding the ending -ak to the cardinal form). The exception to this is nim = " half ", which is perhaps more common than the Arabic form.

The Arabic forms are :—

nesf = *half*	khoms = *fifth*	somn = *eighth*
sols = *third*	sods = *sixth*	tos' = *ninth*
rob' = *quarter*	sob' = *seventh*	oshr = *tenth*

They are used as nouns with the cardinals :—

dô sols = *two-thirds*   sè rob' = *three-quarters*

All the fractions except nim are followed by the Ezâfè when the following noun is definite ; thus nesf-e-shab = " half of the night " (also " midnight ") ; but nim sâ'at = " half an hour ", rob' sâ'at = " a quarter of an hour ".

OTHER NUMERAL FORMS

(58) " times " is expressed by daf'è, bâr, martabè, e.g. " twice " = dô daf'è, " four times " = chahâr martabè. dô martabè and dô bârè also mean "again". These forms may be used for multiplication, or dar or tâ as follows :—

" three times four is twelve " = sè daf'è chahâr davâzdah mishavad, *or* sè dar chahâr . . ., *or* sè chahâr tâ. . . .

" one by one," " two by two," etc., are expressed by repeating the Cardinal : yek yek, dô tâ dô tâ, etc. Compare also sè chahâr (tâ) = " three or four ".

EXERCISE VIII

(1) chahâr nafar kârger lâzem = **I require four labourers to** dâram, in châdor-râ **put up this tent** bezanand

(2) az ân davâzdah nafar kè = **Of those twelve men that we** avval dâshtim, hâlâ faghat **had at first, only three are** sè nafar mândand **left**

(3) bâghiyeshân chè tôr = **What has become of the** shodand ? **rest of them ?**

(4) kâr-râ   mêl   nadâshtand,   = They did not like the work,
raftand shahr   and went to the town

(5) panjâh tâ bil, sizdah tâ = Send fifty spades, thirteen
palang o sè tâ tabar har chè   picks and three axes as
zudtar beferestid   quickly as possible

(6) dar râh be- si tâ lâri bishtar = On the road I passed more
gozashtam   than thirty lorries

(7) shâyad ghâsed-e-shirâz   = Perhaps they were bound for
budand   Shiraz

(8) khabar   dâshtè-im   kè = We have news that the
doshman davist tâ sarbâz   enemy   has   sent   200
taraf-e-shahr ferestâdè ast   soldiers in the direction
                                              of the town

(9) ra'is-e-gomrok   khabar = The Chief Customs Officer
midehad kè dar gomrok sad   informs us that 100 cases
tâ sandugh chây vâred   of tea have arrived in the
shodand   Customs

(10) omidvâr am injâ sè chahâr = I hope you will stay here
ruz digar mimânid   three or four more days

(11) khêli mêl dâshtam, vali = I should very much like to,
mota'assefânè   majbur-am   but unfortunately I am
harakat bokonam, chunkè dô   obliged to go, as I must be
ruz digar bâyad dar âbâdân   in Abadan in two days'
beshavam   time

(12) chand vaght ast dar irân = How long have you been in
hastid ?   Iran ?

(13) faghat sè mâh pish injâ = I came here only three
âmadè am   months ago

(14) pas khêli khob fârsi yâd = Then you have learnt Persian
gereftid   very well

(15) khêr, âghâ, dar London = No, I studied in London for
shesh mâh dars kardam   six months

TIME, DATE, MEASURES, ETC.

(59) THE *Time of Day* is expressed as follows :—

What is the time ?	= sâ'at <u>ch</u>and ast ? (lit. *how much is the hour ?*)
It is four o'clock	= sâ'at-e-<u>ch</u>ahâr ast (lit. *the hour of four*)
It is half-past four	= sâ'at-e-<u>ch</u>ahâr o nim ast (lit. *the hour of four and a half*)
It is a quarter to four	= sâ'at-e-<u>ch</u>ahâr rob' kam ast (lit. *the hour of four quarter less*)
It is five minutes past four	= sâ'at-e-<u>ch</u>ahâr o panj da<u>gh</u>i<u>gh</u>è ast (lit. *the hour of four and five minutes*)

N.B.—" at what time will he come ? " = sâ'at-e-<u>ch</u>and miyâyad ? *or* <u>ch</u>è va<u>gh</u>t miyâyad ?

(60)

second	= sâniyè	*fortnight*	= dô haftè, pânzdah ruz
minute	= da<u>gh</u>i<u>gh</u>è	*month*	= mâh
hour	= sâ'at	*year*	= sâl
day	= ruz	*century*	= <u>gh</u>arn
week	= haftè		

(61) The *Months* of the Iranian solar (<u>sh</u>amsi) year now in use in Iran are :—

farvardin	= 31 *days*	mehr	= 30 *days*
ordibehe<u>sh</u>t	= 31 *days*	âbân	= 30 *days*
<u>kh</u>ordâd	= 31 *days*	âzor	= 30 *days*
tir	= 31 *days*	dê	= 30 *days*
mordâd	= 31 *days*	bahman	= 30 *days*
<u>sh</u>ahrivar	= 31 *days*	esfand	= 29 *days*

N.B.—esfand has 30 days in a leap-year (sâl-e-kabisè). Leap-years occur every four years, except that every eighth leap-year comes after an interval of five years (that is to say, a cycle of eight leap-years takes 33 years instead of 32). The year 1317, which began on 21st March, 1938, was a leap-year (ending on 21st March, 1939), and was the 33rd (last) year of a leap-year cycle. The 1st Farvardin, 1319, was 22nd March, 1940.

N.B.—The above month names (especially the short ones) are usually followed by the word mâh, e.g. tir-mâh, dê-mâh, etc.

The usual forms of the European months are derived from the French.

The Arabic (Moslem) months are not now much used in Iran.

Dates are shown by placing the Ordinals in front of the month with Ezâfè, e.g. Tir 14th = chahârdahom-e-tirmâh.

(62) The *Days of the Week* are :—

(ruz-e-) jom'è	=	*Friday*
(,,) shambè	=	*Saturday*
(,,) yekshambè	=	*Sunday*
(,,) dôshambè	=	*Monday*
(,,) seshambè	=	*Tuesday*
(,,) chahârshambè	=	*Wednesday*
(,,) panjshambè	=	*Thursday*

N.B.—Friday (jom'è), which is the first day of the week, is a holiday.

ANNUAL HOLIDAYS

(63) id-e-nôruz (1st Farvardin) : New Year's Day.
sizdah-e-id-e-nôruz (13th Farvardin).

tavallod-e-vâlâhazrat-e-homâyun (4th Âbân) :   Birthday
of the Crown Prince.

kudêtâ (3rd Esfand) :   *Coup d'état* of 1299.

molûd-e-shâhanshâhi (24th Esfand) :   Birthday of H.I.M.
the Shah.

The following Moslem festivals (whose dates vary from
year to year according to the Moslem calendar [1]) are among
those generally observed :—

Birthday of the Prophet.
Death of the Prophet.
Martyrdom of Ali (ghatl-e-emâm ali).
Id-e-fetr.
Id-e-azhâ.
Martyrdom of Husain (ghatl-e-emâm hosên) (10th and
11th of Moharram).
Martyrdom of Hasan (ghatl-e-emâm hasan).

The *Seasons* are :—

zamestân = *winter*   tabestân = *summer*
behâr   = *spring*   pâ'iz   = *autumn*

(64) *Age* may be expressed in one of the following ways :—

how old are you ? =
{ chand sâl dârid ? (*how many years have you ?*)
  sennatân chand ast ? (*how much is your age ?*) }

I am twenty years old =
{ bist sâl dâram
  sennam bist sâl ast }

---

[1] The Moslem year is lunar (ghamari) (354 days), and these festivals
therefore occur about eleven days earlier each year.

MEASURES

(65) The Metric system is officially used in Iran, but certain older measures have survived in colloquial use.

Length

gerè   = 2·5 in. approx.
ghadam = pace = 8 gerè = 20 in. approx.
zar'⎫
gaz ⎭ = ell = 2 ghadam = 1 metre approx.
farsakh = 6,000 gaz = $3\frac{1}{2}$–$3\frac{3}{4}$ miles

Weight

sir   = $\frac{1}{6}$ lb. approx.
chârak   = 10 sir = $1\frac{2}{3}$ lb. approx.
mann ⎫
bâtmann ⎭ = maund of Tabriz = 4 chârak = $6\frac{2}{3}$ lb. approx.
mann-e-shâh = maund of Isfahan = 2 bâtmann.
kharvâr   = donkey-load = 100 bâtmann = 670 lb.

COINAGE

(66) The official currency is as follows :—

100 dinâr = 1 reyâl (one **rial)**
100 reyâl = 1 pahlavi

The following terms, however, which have survived from before the time of the present regime, are also commonly used.

shâhi   = 5 dinâr
ghrân   = 1 reyâl
tumân = 10 reyâl

The official rate of exchange is normally about 80 reyâl to £1.

The following notes and coins are in use :—

	English *Equivalents.*		
Coins.	£	*s.*	*d.*
5 dinâr .		—	
50 dinâr .			1½
Notes.			
5 reyâl .		1	3
10 reyâl .		2	6
20 reyâl .		5	0
50 reyâl .		12	6
100 reyâl .	1	5	0
200 reyâl .	2	10	0
500 reyâl .	6	5	0
1,000 reyâl .	12	10	0

Other obsolete coins are still found in circulation (ranging
from 1 dinâr upwards). Some of these are in an older currency,
in which there were 1,000 dinâr to the ghrân.

EXERCISE IX

(1) fardâ sobh sâ'at-e-hasht o = **Breakfast is to be ready at**
   rob' nâshtâ hâzer bâshad   **a quarter past eight to-**
                                        morrow morning

(2) ghetâr bist o panj daghighè = **The train has arrived twenty-**
   dir âmadè ast   **five minutes late**

(3) kudetâ sevvom-e-   = **The** *coup d'état* **took place**
   esfandmâh   sâl-e-hazâr o   **on 3rd Esfand, 1299**
   davist o navâd o noh vâghe'
   shod

(4) hivdahom-e-dêmâh sâl-e-   = **On 17th Dey, 1314, the**
   hazâr o sisad o chahârdah   **wearing of the veil was**
   pushidan-e-châdor dar irân   **abolished in Iran**
   mamnu' shod

(5) ruz-e-seshambè târikhesh = What is the date on
    chi-è ?   Tuesday ?

(6) gamân mikonam   = I think it is the 14th
    chahârdahom-e-ordibehesht   Ordibehesht
    ast

(7) velâdatat kê bud ?   = When were you born ?

(8) fe'lan namidânam, âghâ, = Actually I do not know, but
    vali dar shenâsnâmeyam sâl-   my identity certificate says
    e-hazâr o davist o navâd o   1294
    chahâr naveshtè

(9) pas sennat bist o panj sâl = Then you are 25 years old
    ast

(10) sè tâ zar' pârchè-ye-sabz = I want three yards of green
     mikhâham   cloth

(11) In pârchè mâl-e-zhâpan = This cloth is Japanese ; it is
     ast ; ghèmatesh yek zar'   four and a half rials the
     chahâr ghrân o nim ast   yard

(12) dô kilô sheker lâzem = I require two kilos of sugar,
     dâram, nim kilô chây o sè   half a kilo of tea and three-
     rob' kilô ghahvè   quarters of a kilo of
                                 coffee

(13) sheker yek kilô dô ghrân = Sugar is 2 rials the kilo, tea
     ast, chây yek kilo punzdah   15 rials, and coffee 20 rials
     ghrân-è, ghahvè yek kilô
     bist ghrân-è

(14) pas tamâmesh chahâr = Then the total is 4 rials +
     ghrân o haft ghrân o nim o $7\frac{1}{2}$ rials + 15 rials, which
     punzdah ghrân-è, kè bist o   makes $26\frac{1}{2}$ rials
     shesh ghrân o nim mishad

Lesson X

WORD FORMATION

(a) Persian

(67) The formation of verbs has already been discussed in paras. 22, 31, 38–41.

The question of noun and adjective formation is not one which need be studied in great detail by the beginner; at the same time some knowledge of its peculiarities will be found to be very helpful.

There are two main types of compound noun or adjective :—

(68) (a) Those formed from two words placed together with or without a linking letter.

Examples are :—

Two Nouns

ruznâmè	= *newspaper*	mizkhânè	= *dining-room*
teleghrâfkhânè	= *telegraph office*	khâbgâh	= *bedroom*

Noun and Adjective

badbu	= *evil-smelling*	khoshbu	= *sweet-smelling*
chahârpâ	= *quadruped*	marizkhânè	= *hospital*

Preposition and Noun

bifahm	= *stupid*	pishkhedmat	= *butler*

Verbal Stem and Noun

ruzshomâr	= *diary*	âshpaz	= *cook*
istgâh	= *station*	bandshalvâr	= *braces*

ḣokmrân	= governor	bandjurâb	= sock-suspenders
rangzan	= painter	sâ'atsâz	= watchmaker
ḡâliforush	= carpet seller	dastkash	= glove

Two Verbal Stems

goftogu = conversation   jostoju = search
âmadoraft = traffic, coming and going

(69) (b) Those formed from a word with a prefix or suffix.

Examples:—

Prefixes

nâ-	= without, un-	ham-	= together, equal
nâdân	= ignorant	hamrâh	= companion
nâpâk	= dirty	hamvâri	= evenness
nâkhosh	= ill	hamvatan	= compatriot

Suffixes

(a) Nouns

-bân	Occupation	bâḡbân	= gardener
-kâr		âteshkâr	= fire watchman
-ger		âhanger	= blacksmith
-âr	Verbal Noun	raftâr	= behaviour
-âri		gereftâr	= prisoner
-dân	Container	ḡalamdân	= pen-case
-estân	Place of	golestân	= rose garden
		shahrestân	= county
		bimârestân	= hospital
-i	Abstract Noun	mardi	= manliness
		khobi	= goodness
-esh	Verbal Noun	âmuzesh	= learning
		kushesh	= effort
-â	Abstract	garmâ	= heat
		sarmâ	= cold
-ak	Diminutive	inak	= this
		chârak	= quarter (weight)

-chè	Diminutive	darichè	= *window*
-chi {	(Turkish)—	tofangchi	= *watchman*
	Occupation	tayyârechi	= *airman*

(The suffix -chi is disliked by educated speakers.)

(b) Adjectives

-mand	dôlatmand	= *wealthy*
-vâr	omidvâr	= *hopeful*
-ânè	divânè	= *mad*
-i (Relative ending)	irâni	= *Iranian*
-nâk {	khatarnâk	= *dangerous*
	ghazabnâk	= *angry*
-in {	shirin	= *sweet*
	pasin	= *last, latest*
	pâ'in	= *low, at the foot of*
-è {	harruzè	= *daily*
	dômâhè	= *two-monthly*

There are many others which the student will recognize for himself. Many apparent suffixes are really verbal stems, used as in para. 68, e.g. -sâz, -zan, -rân, etc.

THE ARABIC ELEMENT IN PERSIAN

(70) Arabic grammar and syntax has not affected the structure of Persian to any great extent. But its influence on Persian vocabulary has been enormous, and though efforts are being made officially to eliminate Arabic words, it is unlikely that any marked impression will be made on everyday speech (any more than that it has been possible to eliminate Latin from English).

It will be necessary first of all to consider the peculiar method of word formation in Arabic (a method characteristic of all the Semitic languages). In the Indo-European languages (such as English and Persian) words are built up (by means

of suffixes, phonetic changes, etc.), from roots which may at
one time have existed as words, but which have only in rare
cases actually survived, and are of no practical value so far
as the study of grammar is concerned.

The Arabic root is exactly the opposite ; it is purely
theoretical (as will be seen, it consists entirely of consonants),
but it is of the greatest grammatical importance. Once the
root is known, a whole series of words (with fairly well-defined
shades of meaning) may be formed from it according to precise
" mathematical " formulæ.

The majority of Arabic words are formed from triliteral
(three consonant) roots (though some are formed from four).
To these three (or four) consonants are added various vowels
and consonants (or one of them may be doubled). Thus the
word ketâb " book " is formed from the root k-t-b, which
has the basic meaning of " writing " ; forsat " opportunity "
from f-r-s ; lâzem " necessary " from l-z-m, etc. When one
of the consonants is v, y, or ', contraction may take place,
and the root is not then always readily distinguishable ; but
as such contraction is according to regular rules, it does not
really present any difficulty (e.g. bannâ " mason " for bannây,
from root b-n-y ; sâ'at " hour " for sava'at, from root s-v-').

Many Arabic words used in Persian are formed according
to formulæ which have no special importance, and such words
may be learned purely as vocabulary. But there are certain
forms which the student will find it useful to remember.
These will be discussed in the next lesson

EXERCISE X

(1) har vaght farrâsh mâl-e- = **When the messenger from**
    postkhânè   âmad,   in   **the post-office comes, give**
    kâghezhâ-râ besh bedeh   **him these letters**

(2) âg͟hâ, yek g͟hâliforus͟h hâzer = **Sir, a carpet seller is here**
ast, g͟hâlihâ o gelimhâ o   **with some beautiful car-**
pardehâ-ye-g͟has͟hang dârad   **pets, geleems and curtains**

(3) bes͟h bogu, emruz kâr = **Tell him, to-day I am busy,**
dâram, namitavânam c͟hizi   **I cannot buy anything**
bek͟haram

(4) s͟hâyad, agar fardâ âmad, = **Perhaps if he comes to-**
vag͟ht k͟hâham dâs͟ht ;   **morrow I shall have time ;**
mibinam   **I will see**

(5) diruz   az   edârè-ye- = **Yesterday I asked for a**
estek͟hdâm yek âhanger   **blacksmith from the**
k͟hâstam, ammâ hanuz   **Labour Office, but he has**
nayâmadè   **not yet come**

(6) k͟hêli mos͟hkel ast artizânhâ- = **It is very difficult for us to**
râ pêdâ bokonim   **find artisans**

(7) âg͟hâ-ye-sar-amalè, sè nafar = **Foreman, take three labour-**
kârger begir, va ân lulehâ   **ers and carry those pipes**
be-kârk͟hânè bebar   **to the workshop**

(8) bes͟h goftam be-mariz- = **I told him to go to the**
k͟hânè borô, g͟habul nakard **hospital, but he refused**

(9) dar môg͟he'-i kè ruznâmè = **At the moment when I**
vâz kardam, telfon zang   **opened the newspaper, the**
zadè   **telephone rang**

(10) c͟hand nafar âtes͟hkâr dar = **How many fire watchmen**
tasfiyek͟hânè dârand ?   **have they in the refinery ?**

(11) namidânam, vali yag͟hin = **I do not know, but I am**
dâram har vag͟ht o har kojâ **sure that whenever and**
âtes͟h zadè, zud pêdâ mis͟had **wherever a fire may break**
                             out, it will soon be dis-
                             discovered

WORD FORMATION

(b) Arabic

(71) In describing the various forms, the three consonants f-s-l will be used to indicate the three root consonants; any letters in addition to these are part of the particular "formula". Thus the word forsat would be said to be of the form foslat; it must be understood that the formulæ themselves have not necessarily any meaning.

N.B.—The three "token" consonants used by Arab and Iranian grammarians are f-'-l, but the second of these is obviously not suitable for English students. However, it may be found that native teachers will use them.

Noun Forms

(72) (a) fassâl is used commonly for trades and occupations, e.g. :—

naghghâsh	(n-gh-sh)	= *painter*
baghghâl	(b-gh-l)	= *grocer*
najjâr	(n-j-r)	= *carpenter*
bannâ	(b-n-y)	= *builder, mason*
farrâsh	(f-r-sh)	= *messenger*

(b) Nouns of Place and Time have the prefix ma-, e.g. :—

manzel	(n-z-l)	= *house*
madrasè	(d-r-s)	= *school*
martabè	(r-t-b)	= *time*

(c) Nouns of Instrument have the prefix me-, e.g. :—

meftâh	(f-t-h)	= *key*

(d) By far the most important group of noun formulæ,
however, is the so-called Broken Plural. The majority of
Arabic Plurals are formed, not by the addition of a termination, but by an internal change in the word, that is, by the
use of another formula. Unfortunately there is very little
connection (in most cases) between the formula used for the
singular noun and that used for its plural; it cannot even
be said that certain formulæ are reserved for use as plurals.
The correct use of the Arabic Broken Plural must, therefore,
be largely a matter of learning vocabulary; however, some of
the commoner forms are given below as a guide.

(a) fosul :—

hadd	*limit*	(h-d-d)	hodud
amr	*affair*	('-m-r)	omur

(b) afsâl :—

vaght	*time*	(v-gh-t)	ôghât (for avghât)
shakhs	*person*	(sh-kh-s)	ashkhâs
sâheb	*owner*	(s-h-b)	ashâb

Certain plurals of this form are used with a singular
meaning in Persian, e.g. :—

arbâb (r-b-b) *master* (Sing. rabb = *Lord* (*God*))
anbâr (n-b-r) *store* (Sing. nibr (Ar.) = *barn*)
asbâb (s-b-b) *tool* (Sing. sabab = *cause, means*)

(c) fosalâ (esp. from the singular form fasil) :—

amir	*prince, commander*	('-m-r) omarâ
ra'is	*chief, head*	(r-'-s) ro'asâ
shâ'er	*poet*	(sh-'-r) sho'arâ

(d) fasâyel, favâsel, favâsil, mafâsel, mafâsil (and similar
forms for words with four root letters), e.g. :—

lâzemè	*necessary*	(l-z-m)	lavâzem
shart	*condition*	(sh-r-t)	sharâyet

masjed *mosque*	(s-j-d)	masâjed
ghânun *law*	(gh-n-n)	ghavânin
dokkân *shop*	(d-k-k-n)	dakâkin

There are, of course, many other forms which must be learnt as they are met. It should be noted that all these forms are regarded in Arabic as feminine singular, and therefore when they are qualified by an Arabic adjective, the latter should take the Arabic feminine ending -è (see para. 8). This rule is not always observed except in careful speech.

In uneducated colloquial the Persian plural is often used even when an Arabic plural is required.

Verbal Forms

(73) From any given root a large number of different forms of the verb may be formed, each with different shades of meaning connected with the original one. The total number of forms possible is fifteen, but only nine of these are common, and no one root even has all of these. Each form, of course, has a full complement of tenses, participles, and so on, but the only parts in common use in Persian are Verbal Nouns and Participles.

(a) The former are especially common in the compound verbs. For those formed from the First Form no rule can be given; examples are : ghatl (gh-t-l) = " killing " ; fohsh (f-h-sh) = " abuse " ; shekâyat (sh-k-y) = " complaint ".

However, from the other forms (the so-called Derived Forms) the Verbal Nouns are regular, and are formed as follows :—

II. tafsil,	e.g. ta'til	('-t-l)	= *holiday*
III. mofâsalè,	e.g. molâhaze	(l-h-z)	= *attention*
IV. efsâl,	e.g. ekhrâj	(kh-r-j)	= *expulsion*
V. tafassol,	e.g. tasavvor	(s-v-r)	= *imagination*

VI.	tafâsol,	e.g. ta'ârof	('-r-f)	= *offer*
VII.	enfesâl,	e.g. enhesâr	(h-s-r)	= *monopoly*
VIII.	eftesâl,	e.g. e<u>sh</u>tebâh	(<u>sh</u>-b-h)	= *mistake*
IX.	Rare			
X.	estefsâl,	e.g. este'mâl	('-m-l)	= *use*

(*b*) Similarly two *Participles* (Present and Past) may be formed from each form, as follows :—

	Present.	Past.	Example.	Root.
I.	fâsel	mafsul	{ <u>sh</u>â'er *poet*	<u>sh</u>-'-r
			{ ma<u>sh</u>mul *conscripted*	<u>sh</u>-m-l
II.	mofassel	. . . al	mofatte<u>sh</u> *inspector*	f-t-<u>sh</u>
III.	mofâsel	. . . al	mo'âven *assistant*	'-v-n
IV.	mofsel	. . . al	mo<u>sh</u>kel *difficult*	<u>sh</u>-k-l
V.	motafassel	. . . al	mota<u>sh</u>akker *thankful*	<u>sh</u>-k-r
VI.	motafâsel	. . . al	motahâreb *belligerent*	h-r-b
VII.	monfasel	. . . al	monfajar *exploded*	f-j-r
VIII.	moftasel	. . . al	moltafet *attentive*	l-f-t
IX.	Rare			
X.	mostafsel	. . . al	mosta<u>kh</u>dem *employee*	<u>kh</u>-d-m

In all but the First Form, the only difference between Present and Past is the vowel-change in the last syllable.

When the last two root letters are the same, or when one of the letters is v or y, certain changes (by contraction) may take place; the rules for these need not be learnt, but a few illustrations will be useful.

Verbal Nouns

efsâl	t-y-'	etâ'at (for etyâ'(at))	= *obedience*
	d-y-'	edâ (for edyâ')	= *payment*
eftesâl	v-k-'	ettekâ (for evtekâ')	= *support*
estefsâl	'-f-v	este'fâ (for este'fâv)	= *resignation*

Participles

mafsul	v-l-d	môlud (for mavlud)	= *birth*
mofsel	d-v-r	modir (for modver)	= *director*
	n-sh-'	mon<u>sh</u>i (for mon<u>sh</u>e')	= *clerk*
monfasal	h-l-l	monhall (for monhalal)	= *demobilized*
mostafsal	r-v-h	mostarâh (for mostarvah)	= *W.C.*

NUMERAL FORMS

(74) These have already been mentioned in paras. 56, 57. It will be seen that all the fractions are of the form fosl, and the Arabic Ordinals of the form fâsel.

ARABIC TERMINATIONS

(75) Most of the Arabic case-endings have been lost; a few, however, are of importance.

(*a*) The Feminine ending -atun. The case-ending -un (in Arabic) is normally dropped, and the ending then becomes -a, except before a vowel, when the t reappears. In Persian, however, the ending either becomes -è, in which case the t is lost altogether, or -at, in which case the t is always retained.

(*b*) The Dual ending -ên (for two). It is found in such words as vâledên = " parents ". (Sing. vâled.)

(*c*) The " Sound " Plural ending -ín (Masc.), -ât (Fem.), found especially with Arabic participles, e.g. mohandesin (h-n-d-s) = " engineers, surveyors ". (Sing. mohandes.)

(*d*) The Accusative Singular ending -an, used adverbially, e.g. ta<u>gh</u>riban = " nearly " (see para. 33).

(76) A few Arabic expressions are used in their entirety without change, e.g. :—

ya'ni   = *that is to say* (lit. *it means*)
belhaghighè = *actually* (lit. *in the truth*)
foghalâdè   = *extra* (lit. *above the custom*)
salâm alêkom = (Moslem greeting—lit. *peace upon you*)
ba'd-ez-zohr = *afternoon* (lit. *after the noon*)
bênalmelal-i = *international* (lit. *between the nations* +
               Relative ending)

EXERCISE XI

(1) in kot va ân shalvâr be- = Take this coat and those
    khayyât bebarid, yek khordè   trousers to the tailor, they
    pârè shodè   are a little torn

(2) momken ast masâjed-e- = Is it possible for me to visit
    irân zeyârat bokonam ?   the mosques of Iran ?

(3) masâjed-e-esfahân-râ barâ- = They have opened the
    ye-zeyârat vâz kardand   mosques of Isfahan for
                                   visiting

(4) shoghlatân najjâr bud, = You were employed as a
    hoghugh chand gereftid ?   carpenter, what were your
                                 wages ?

(5) dar esfahân dokkân-e- = In Isfahan I had a private
    shakhsi dâshtam, har ruz   shop and I made about 5
    taghriban panj tumân   tumans daily
    gereftam

(6) vaghti kè pish-e-sherkat = When I worked for the
    kâr kardam, mavâjebam   company, my wages were
    ruzè bist ghrân bud   20 rials a day

(7) vozarâ-ye-mokhtâr-e- = The ambassadors of the
    kashvarhâ-ye-donyâ hâzer   nations of the world were
    budand   present

(8) emruz id-e-ghatl-e-emâm- = To-day it is the festival of
    hosên ast   the murder of Hosain

(9) forukhtan-e-sigâri dar irân = The sale of cigarettes in Iran
    zir-e-dast-e-enhesâri ast   is in the hands of a
                                  monopoly

(10) az in manzelhâ kodâm = Which of these houses do
     mêl dârid ?   you prefer ?

(11) ekhteyâr nadâram, âghâ ; = I have no choice, sir ;
     har kodâm befarmâ-id   whichever you order

(12) ta'ajjob mikonam in = I am surprised that no one
     eshtebâh hichkas nadidè   has seen this mistake

(77) GREETINGS, OATHS, HONORIFICS, POLITE PHRASES, ETC.

salâm alêkom	= *Peace be upon you* (Moslem greeting)
alêkom-os-salâm	= *Upon you be peace* (Answer)
shâdzi	(Modern greeting)
ahvâl-e-sharif (chè tôr ast ?)	= *How are you ?*
al-hamdo-lêllâh az eltefât-e-shomâ	= *Praise be to God for your kindness*
khodâ hâfez(-e-shomâ)	= *Good-bye* (familiar)
marhamat zeyâd	= *Good-bye* (formal)
morakhkhasam ?	(said by visitor when leaving)
sobh(-e-shomâ) be-khêr	= *Good morning*
shab(-e-shomâ) be-khêr	= *Good night*
shâd bâsh	(greeting at New Year, etc.)
zandè bâsh	= *Long live . . . ! Viva !*
salâmati	= *Good health !*

(78) OATHS AND INTERJECTIONS

be-khodâ ghasam	
jân-e-shomâ	} Oaths of " Conviction "
jân-e-man, -e-khodam	
yâllâh	= *Hurry up !* etc.
bakh bakh	
âferin	} = *Bravo ! Well done !*
bârakâllâh	

pedar sag	
pedar su<u>kh</u>tè	
pedarat nâ-mard	Terms of abuse
harâmzâdè	

en<u>sh</u>âllâh	= *If it please God* (surprise; lit.
mâ<u>sh</u>âllâh	*What God wills*)
besmellâh	= *In the name of God !* (said before meals or before undertaking any project)
al-hamdo-lellâh	= *Praise to God !* (thankfulness)

HONORIFICS AND TITLES

(79) The lavish use of honorifics and titles which was characteristic of the older Persian language is rapidly dying out, partly through contact with Western ideas, and partly as the result of direct encouragement by the educational authorities. There are, however, various expressions and turns of phrase which the student will do well to learn, as without them his speech will appear uneducated and boorish.

As a rule the Personal Pronouns are not used by speakers of each other in polite conversations between equals, or in addressing a superior. The following expressions may be used for the 2nd Person :—

jenâb-e-âli
sarkâr-e-âli *rather formal*
hazrat-e-âli
<u>gh</u>orbân(-e-tô, -e-<u>sh</u>omâ) *familiar*

The usual substitute for the 1st Person is bandè, literally " bound ", i.e. " slave, servant ".

Terms of affection are numerous, examples being :—

$\left.\begin{array}{l}\text{pedar-jân}\\\text{jân-e-pedar}\end{array}\right\} = $ *soul of your father*

jânam   = *my soul*, etc.

(80) *Terms of Respect* : in speaking to a man, the word âg͟hâ " Mr.", " sir " is used ; to a woman, k͟hânom. " Ladies and Gentlemen " = âg͟hâyân va k͟hânomhâ.

The word âg͟hâ is prefixed to all titles except those of high rank, e.g. âg͟hâ-ye-doktor, âg͟hâ-ye-hokumat " Governor ", etc. For officers of the lower ranks, the correct title is sarkâr, for those of higher ranks, timsâr. Ministers and persons of similar status are addressed as jenâb, followed by the appropriate title. The word jenâb, however, is generally used whenever addressing a superior, whatever his rank, e.g. jenâb-e-ra'is. The Royal Family are addressed as follows :

H.I.M. the Shah	= pis͟hgâh-e-a'lâhazrat-e-homâyun-e-s͟hâhans͟hâhi
H.I.M. the Queen	= pis͟hgâh-e-olyâhazrat malekè-ye-irân
The Crown Prince	= pis͟hgâh - e - vâlâhazrat - e - homâ-yunivali'ahd-e-irân
Other sons of the Shah	= vâlâhazrat (+ name)
Other daughters of the Shah	= olyâhazrat (+ name)

POLITE PHRASES

(81) It is common, in polite conversation, to substitute for the auxiliary part of the compound verb, especially for kardan, the verb farmudan (lit. command). Thus for ejâzè dâdan is said ejâzè farmudan, for mêl dâs͟htan—mêl farmudan, for molâhazè kardan—molâhazè farmudan, etc. There are numerous other examples.

The word farmudan is also used by itself with the
meaning of " say " ; <u>ch</u>è farmudid = " what did you say ? "
Examples of other polite periphrases are as follows :—

moltafet <u>sh</u>odid ?	= *Do you understand ?*
fôt <u>sh</u>od	= *He has passed away*
bi zahmat, befarmâ-id	= *Please*
mamnun, -am, -e-<u>sh</u>omâ, mota<u>sh</u>akker	= *Thank you*
beba<u>kh</u>shid	= *Excuse me*
mamnun, <u>ch</u>a<u>sh</u>m, etâ'at mikonam (by a servant)	= *Very well, certainly*
<u>ch</u>erâ ! albattè	= *Certainly, of course*
<u>kh</u>êli <u>kh</u>ob, besyâr <u>kh</u>ob	= *Very well*
<u>kh</u>êli zahmat dâdam (said by a visitor when leaving)	= *I have given you much trouble*
<u>kh</u>êli <u>kh</u>o<u>sh</u> âmadid ; az zeyârat - e - <u>sh</u>omâ <u>kh</u>êli <u>kh</u>o<u>sh</u>va<u>gh</u>t <u>sh</u>odam, va hi<u>ch</u> zahmat nabud	= *You have been very welcome*
kêf-e-<u>sh</u>omâ, mêl-e-<u>sh</u>omâ	= *As you wish*
fekr-e-<u>sh</u>omâ	= *As you think*
â<u>gh</u>â-ye-emâmi {ta<u>sh</u>rif / dârand ? / hastand ?}	= *Is Mr. Emami present ?*
<u>kh</u>êr, â<u>gh</u>â, ta<u>sh</u>rif nadârand, ta<u>sh</u>rif bordand	= *No, sir, he is not here, he has gone away*
fardâ ta<u>sh</u>rif miyâvarand	= *He will come to-morrow*

arz kardan is used to introduce statements, etc., as the
following examples show :—

arz mikonam (be-<u>kh</u>edmat-e-<u>sh</u>omâ) kè ...	= *I would like to say that ...*
<u>ch</u>è farmudid ?	= *What did you say ?*

arz nakardam	=	*I did not speak*
chè arz konam ?	=	*What shall I say ?*
bandè chè midânam ?	=	*How should I know ?*
mota'assef-am	=	*I am sorry*
khâhesh mikonam	=	*I request*
êb nadârad (nist)	=	*It doesn't matter*
khêli ôghâtesh talkh shod	=	*He was very angry, upset*
marhamat befarmâ-id	=	*Will you be so kind as to . . .* *Will you do me the pleasure* *of . . .*

EXERCISE XII

(1) jenâb-e-arbâbat tashrif dârand ? = Is your master at home ?

(2) balè, âghâ, tashrif dârand ; befarmâ-id tâ besh khabar bedam = Yes, sir, he is here ; please come in while I inform him

(3) salâm alêkom âghâ ; chè tôr hastid ? = Greetings ! How are you ?

(4) al-hamdo-lellah az eltefât-e-jenâb-e-âli, emruz hâlam khob shod = Thank you for asking, to-day I feel quite well

(5) yek khordè chây mêl mifarmâ-id ? = Would you like a little tea ?

(6) dar shahr chè khabar-è ? = What is the news in the town ?

(7) bandè dô haftè rokhsat gereftam, diruz faghat bar gashtam = I took two weeks' leave, I only returned yesterday

(8) khâheshmand am zud pish-e-bandè tashrif beyârid = I hope you will come and visit me soon

(9) khêli motashakker-e-sarkâr- = Thank you very much ; I
    e-âli hastam ; enshâllâh dô   hope I shall come in two
    sè ruz digar miyâyam   or three days

(10) jân-e-shomâ, âghâ, hâlâ sè = I assure you it is three
    mâh ast hichkas zeyârat-e-   months since anyone
    man nayâmadè ast   visited me

(11) hâlâ ejâzè midid,   = Now I must leave you
    morakhkhas misham ?

(12) marhamat zeyâd âghâ ; = Good-bye ; I hope you will
    enshâllâh zud bar gashtid   soon be back

CONVERSATIONS

TRAVELLING

âghâ, mêl dâram be-esfahân = I want to go to Isfahan :
beravam ; chè tôr mishad ?   how can it be done ?

mikhâhid be-tâksi beravid yâ = Do you want to go by taxi
be-shârâbân ?   or by charabanc ?

kerâye-e-tâksi chand-è ?   = What is the hire of a taxi ?

emruz ba'd az zohr yek tâksi = A taxi is going this afternoon
harakat mikonad, tush jâ   in which there is room
hast

kerâye-e-yek jâ haftâd o panj = The hire of one seat is 75
reyâl ast   rials

ammâ namitavânam emruz = But I cannot start to-day
harakat konam

pas, agar yek tâksi tamâm = Then, if you want a whole
lâzem dârid, kerâyesh sisad   taxi to yourself, the hire
reyâl mishad   will be 300 rials.

fardâ shârâbân nist ?   = Isn't there a charabanc to-
morrow ?

cherâ, shârâban hast; kerâye-e- = Yes, there is a charabanc ;
yek jâ faghat bist reyâl ast.   the cost of one seat is only
vali râhat nist   20 rials. But it is not
comfortable

êb nadârad ; yek jâ dâkhelesh = Never mind ; reserve one
bar-e-man negâh dârid   seat in it for me

besyâr khob, âghâ ; fardâ = Very well, sir ; it will start
sâ'at-e-noh harakat khâhad   to-morrow at nine o'clock
kard

sar-e-râh — *On the road*

jâ-ye-man kojâ-st ? diruz negâhesh dâshtam	Where is my place ? I reserved it yesterday
in ast, âghâ ; asâsiyetân kojâ-st ?	This is it, sir ; where is your luggage ?
khêli sangin ast, âghâ ; shâyad namishad	It is very heavy ; perhaps it can't be managed
enshâllâh jâ pêdâ mishad	I think there will be room
shârâbân chè vaght miravad ?	What time does the chara--banc go ?
al'ân harakat mikonad, âghâ.	It is going directly, Sir
âghâ-ye-shôfer, mêl dâram yek khordè bekhâbam ; vaghti kè jâ-i rasidim, bi zahmat bidâram bokonid	Driver, I want to go to sleep for a little ; when we have arrived somewhere, please wake me
ân masjed-e-ghashangi kè taraf-e-râst mibinid masjed-e-ghom ast	That beautiful mosque which you see on the right is the mosque of Qum
hâlâ kè sar-e-in kuh âmadim, mitunid shahr-e-esfahân-râ pâ'in bebinid	Now that we have come to the top of this hill, you can see the town of Isfahan below
âghâ, behtarin-e-mehmân-khânè kodâm-è ?	Which is the best hotel ?
in doroshkè begirid ; sâhebesh pish-e-yek mehmânkhânè-ye-khob shomâ-râ mibarad	Take this droshky ; its owner will take you to a good hotel

SIGHTSEEING

âghâ, emruz `mêl dâram masâjed-e-esfahân bebinam	To-day I want to see the mosques of Isfahan
khêli khob âghâ ; yek doroshkè	Very well, sir ; get a droshky

CONVERSATIONS

91

begirid, kè shomâ-râ be mèdân-e-shâh bebarad	to take you to the Maidan-e-Shah
ân masjed-e-bozorg esmesh chi-è ?	What is the name of that big mosque
in masjed-e-shâh esmesh-è ; mêl dârid berid tu ?	That is called the Masjed-e-Shah ; would you like to go inside ?
zinatesh âbi o sabz o zard kheli ghashang-è	Its blue and green and yellow decoration is very beautiful
balè, âghâ ; migand zir-e-dast-e-shâh abbâs sâkhtè shod	Yes, sir ; they say it was built in the time of Shah Abbas
dast-e-râst yek amârat hast, esmesh âli ghâpu-st	On the right is a building called the " Ali Ghapu "
ânjâ chè chiz vâghe' shod ?	What happened there ?
migand ruz-e-id shâh khodesh bâ omarâyesh o vozarâyesh ânjâ neshast	They say that on festivals the Shah sat there with his princes and ministers
un bâb-e-bozorg mâl-e-chi-è ?	What is that big gate there ?
un mâl-e-bâzâr-e-bozorg ast	That belongs to the great bazaar
balè, az in bâzâr khabar dâshtam ; khêli mêl dâram zeyârat konam	Yes, I have heard of this bazaar ; I should very much like to visit it
tulesh namidânam chè ghadr-è ; hamesh zir-e-yek bâm-è	I don't know how long it is ; it is all under one roof
injâ bâzâr-e-masgerân-è, va az ân taraf najjârhâ pêdâ mikonid	Here is the bazaar of the coppersmiths, and over there you will find the carpenters
pas har san'at jâ-ye-khodesh dârad	Then each trade has its own place

mêl dârid yek chizi bekharid ? = Would you like to buy some-
noghrè hast ya talâ, yâ   thing ? There is silver or
shâyad naghshè dust dârid ?   gold, or perhaps you like
                          painting ?

khêli mamnun-e-shomâ hastam, = Thank you very much, but
vali emruz pulam nayâvar-   I have not brought any
dam ; enshâllâh fardâ bar   money to-day ; perhaps I
migardam   will come back to-morrow

SHOPPING

sobh-e-shomâ be-khêr, âghâ ; = Good morning, sir ; what
chè lâzem dârid ?   would you like ?

avval namak o chây o ârd = First I should like some salt
mikhâham   and tea and flour

be-farmâ-id, âghâ, hâzer shod = Here you are, sir, it is ready

in chây mâl-e-kojâ-st ? = Where is this tea from ?

mâl-e-hendostân ast ; ghêma- = It is from India ; the price
tesh khêli boland shod, az   has gone up a lot, on
sabab-e-mâliyât   account of the tax

dô tâ nân-e-tâzè ham bedehid = Also give me two new loaves

janâb-e-âli khodetân mibari- = Will you take them yourself
desh yâ beferestam ?   or shall I send them ?

bi zahmat beferestid, chun kè = Please send them, as I have
mâshin-e-man hâzer nadâ-   not got my car
ram

ghassâbi kojâ hast ?   = Where is there a butcher ?

az ân taraf tashrif bebarid, = Go in that direction, sir,
âghâ, dar kheyâbân-e-shâh   there is one in Shah Street
yeki hast

âghâ, tashrif beyârid tu ; chand = Come inside, sir ; I have
tâ asbâb-e-gharib dâram,   some unusual things to
mikhâham be-hazrat-e-âli   show you
neshân bedeham

chè chiz dârid, âghâ ? mêl nadâram chizi bekharam	= What have you got ? I don't want to buy anything
âghâ, in ghâli mâl-e-kâshân-è ; namibinid chè tôr bârik-è ?	= This carpet, sir, is from Kashan ; do you see how fine it is ?
in hamesh az abrisham sâkhtè shod	= It is made entirely of silk
chizi gharib ast, âghâ ; vali gamân mikonam ghêmatesh zeyâd-è	= It is wonderful ; but I think its price is too much
eb nadârad, âghâ ; har chè befarmâ-id, ghêmatesh bar-e-shomâ dorost mikonam	= It doesn't matter, sir ; whatever you say, I will make its price all right for you
momken ast yek chizi arzântar az in neshân bedid ?	= Can you show me anything cheaper than this ?
chashm, âghâ ; in pârchehâ molâhazè be-farmâ-id	= Very good, sir ; please look at these pieces of cloth
in chè tôr dorost mikonand ?	= How do they make this ?
in kâr-e-khosusi-ye-esfahân ast ; naghghâshi bâ dast tasvir mikonad o rangesh mizanad	= This is special Isfahan work ; it is hand-drawn and painted by an artist
ghêmatesh har yek dah tumân ast	= The price is 100 rials each
mâshâllah ! bishtar az panj tuman namideham	= What ! I will not give more than 50 rials
âghâ, khodam noh tumân dâdam, vali êb nadârad, haft tumân ghabul mikonam	= Sir, I gave 90 rials myself ; but never mind, I will accept 70
khêli khob, dô tâ migiram, davâzdah tumân mideham	= All right, I will take two, and give you 120 rials.
besyâr khob âghâ ; marhamat zeyâd	= Very well sir ; good-bye

Domestic

âghâ, châyatân hâzer ast = Sir, your tea is ready

sâ'at chand-è ? cherâ sar-e-vaght nayâvardid ? = What is the time ? Why haven't you brought it in time ?

âghâ, taghsir-e-khodam nabud; môghe'i kè âb pokhtè shod, ketri oftâdè ast o hamesh ru-ye-zamin rikhtè shod = Sir, it is not my fault ; just when the water had boiled the kettle was upset and it was all spilt on the ground

rezâ, vaghti kè nâshtâ khalâs shod, beyid pish-e-man, o fehrest mâl-e-bâzâr mikhânam = Reza, when breakfast is finished, come to me and I will read you the shopping list

chashm, khânom ; hesâb mâl-e-haftè-ye-gozashtè ham bedeham ? = Very well, madam ; shall I give you last week's account as well ?

in chè ghadr zeyâd shod ! sababesh chi-è ? = This has gone up a lot ; why is that ?

chè midânam, khânom ? dar bâzâr hamè chiz ghêmatesh zeyâd shod = How should I know, madam ? Everything has gone up in the bazaar

hâlâ zud berid bâzâr, yek morgh beyârid, o har chè sabzi-ye-khob gir miyâd = Now go at once to the bazaar, and bring a chicken and whatever good vegetables are to be had

emshab mehmân darim, bâyad hamè chiz pâk o ghashang bâshad = This evening we have guests ; everything must be clean and nice

balè, khânom ; al'ân be-âshpaz khabar midam. chand nafar mehmân tashrif miyârand ? = Yes, madam ; I will tell the cook at once. How many guests will there be ?

enshâllâh chahâr nafar miyând = Four people are coming

agar khânom hast, chand tâ gol = If there are ladies, I will get
az bâghbân migiram, o miz- some flowers from the
râ tamyiz mikonam gardener, and decorate the
 table

ân golhâ-ye-tâzè-i-râ kè = Has the gardener planted
arbâbatân âvardè, hanuz those new flowers which
bâghbân kâshtè yâ na ? your master bought ?

balè, khânom, emruz sobh tu = Yes, madam, I saw him this
bâgh didamesh, untaraf-e- morning in the garden ;
chaman kâshtè shod they are planted on the
 far side of the lawn

un farrâsh chè chiz dârad ? = What is the matter with the
cherâ sedâ mikonad ? house-boy ? Why is he
 shouting ?

khânom, bâ ashpâz da'vâ = He is fighting with the cook ;
mikonad ; namidânam chi-è I don't know what is the
 matter

pas besh begid beyâd tu, kâresh = Then tell him to come in
bokonad ; ru-ye-in miz khâk and do his work ; there is
khêli hast a lot of dust on this table

âghâ, chizi mêl dârid ? = Would you like anything,
 sir ?

balè, yek shishè âb-e-jô beyârid = Yes, bring me a glass of beer

IN THE OFFICE

tô, farrâsh, ghalam o khoshk- = Boy, where have you put my
kon mâl-e-man kojâ pen and blotting-paper ?
gozâshti ?

ghalam tu khânè-ye-miz-e- = The pen is in the drawer of
tahrir ast, âghâ ; khoshk- the desk ; I will bring
kon-e-tâzè al'ân miyâram some clean blotting-paper
 immediately

hâlâ be-âghâ-ye-ârâm salâm bedeh = Now go and call Mr. Aram

âghâ-ye-ârâm, diruz khatti be-ra'is-e-shahrabâni ferestâdam ; sevâdesh hâzcr dârid yâ na ? = Mr. Aram, yesterday I sent a letter to the Chief of Police ; have you got a copy of it here ?

maghsud-e-janâb-e-âli kodâm-è ? = Which one do you mean, sir ?

ân kè naveshtamesh, râje' be-mas'alè-ye-nezâm-e-vazifè ; yâd dârid ? = The one I wrote about the question of conscription ; do you remember ?

balè, âghâ, dar daftar gozâshtam ; harchè zudtar pedâsh mikonam o miyâram = Yes, sir, I filed it ; I will find it and bring it as quickly as possible

ân mâshin-navis-i kè tâzè âmadè ast kâresh chè tôr ast ? = How is the work of that typist who has recently come ?

bad nist, âghâ ; vali tajrebè nadârad = She is not bad, but she has had no experience

gamân mikonam faghat sè mâh yâd gereftè ast = I think she has only learnt for three months

âghâ, chand nafar âmadand, migand arizè dârand = Sir, there are some people here who say they have applications

besyâr khob ; yek khordè sabr konand, al'ân yek yeki mibinam = Very well ; let them wait a little, and presently I will see them one by one

khob, shomâ chè kâr dârid ? = Now, what is your business ?

âghâ, man najjâr hastam, dar esfahân dokkân dâshtam ; ba'd shanidam in sherkat najjârhâ lâzem dâsht o âmadam = Sir, I am a carpenter who had a shop in Isfahan ; I heard that this company wanted carpenters, so I came

hâlâ najjarhâ khêli lâzem = **We do not need many**
nadârim; dokkânatân cherâ   **carpenters just now ; why**
forukhtid ?   **did you sell your shop ?**

âghâ naforukhtam ; be-dast-e- = **I didn't sell it ; I handed it**
yek rafigh mâl-e-man dâdam   **over to a friend of mine**

pas injâ mavâjebatân ruzè = **Well, your wages here will**
punzdah ghrân mishad,   **be 15 Rls. a day, not**
bishtar na   **more**

âghâ, man najjâr-e-khob = **Sir, I am a good carpenter ;**
hastam ; agar bishtar az ân   **if I can't get more than**
nagereftam, be-velâyatam   **that, I will go home**
bar gashtam

shomâ chè mikhid ?   = **What do you want ?**

janâb-e-ra'is, har kâri bâshad = **Sir, give me any work there**
bedeh ;   bandè   faghir   **is ; I am poor and have**
hastam, zan o bachè dâram   **a wife and child**

kârat chi-è ?   = **What is your occupation ?**

âghâ, be-khodâ ghasam, hich = **Sir, I have no trade ; if**
kâri balad nistam ; kâr-e-   **there is work for a**
hammâl agar hast, bedeh   **labourer, give it me**

An Investigation

shâhed-e-in hâdesè ki bud ? = **Who   witnessed   this**
                                  accident ?

man hâzer budam, âghâ ; sar-= **I was present, sir ; I was on**
e-râh budam, o mâshin-râ   **the road, and saw the car**
didam

khob, esmatân chi-è, kojâ kâr = **All right, what is your name**
mikonid ?   **and where do you work ?**

esmam gholâm rezâ pesar- = **My name is Gholam Reza,**
e-gholâm hosên ast, dar   **son of Gholam Hosain,**
kârkhânè-ye-sherkat mikan-   **and I am a fitter in the**
ik hastam   **Company's workshop**

98 CONVERSATIONS

pas, râje' be-in hâdesè, chè = Now what happened about
shod ? this accident ?

âghâ, sut zadè bud, bandè = The whistle had gone, I
kâram khalâs kardam, finished my work and was
ghâsed-e-manzelam budam on my way home

manzelatân fe'lan kojâ-st ? = Where is your house
actually ?

sar-e-kuh ast, âghâ, un taraf-e- = It is at the top of the hill,
mêdân sir, on the other side of
the plain

môghe'i kè az ân pichi gashtam = Just when I had turned the
kè moghâbel-e-edârè-ye- corner opposite the
sherkat ast, yek mâshin company's office, I saw a
didam khêli tund miyâmad car coming very fast

shôferesh shenâkhtid ? = Did you recognize its driver ?

khêr, âghâ, kheyâl mikonam = No, sir ; I don't think he
mâl-e-injâ nabud was from here

nâgahân yek nafar meyun-e- = Suddenly I saw a man in the
râh didam ; shenâkhtamesh, middle of the road. I
monshi mâl-e-sherkat bud recognized him as a
company clerk

mashin-râ nadid ? = Didn't he see the car ?

fekr mikonam nadidesh ; dar = I don't think he did ; he
meyân-e-râh gardesh mikard was walking in the middle
of the road

mâshin zud âmadè o besh zadè = The car came quickly and
struck him

ba'd chè kard ? = What did it do then ?

hich tavaghghof nakard, zud = It did not stop at all, but
harakat kard o raft moved off quickly and
disappeared

shomâ khodatân chè kâr = What did you yourself do ?
kardid ?

monshi-râ didam dastesh zakhm khordè, ammâ zeyâd nabud	= I saw that the clerk had hurt his hand, but it was not serious
yek âzhân mâl-e-shahrabâni âmadè ast, besh khabar dâdam, chè vâghe' shod	= A policeman came along, and I told him what had happened
âghâ-ye-hazâr, shomâ ân monshi-ye-sherkat hastid ; be-mâ begid kè in mâshin chè tôr ast betân zadè	= Mr. Hazar, you are the company's clerk ; will you explain to us how this car struck you ?
namidânam, âghâ ; hich nadi-dam tâ mashin âmadè ast	= I don't know, sir ; I saw nothing till the car came
ma'lum shod taghsir-e-ân shôferi-st, kè hichkas nashenâkhtesh	= It is obviously the fault of that driver whom nobody recognized

AT WORK

chand nafar kârger hâzer shodand ?	= How many workmen are here ?
faghat bist o panj tâ âmadand ; un sè tâ digar sar-e-vaght narasidand	= Only twenty-five have come ; those other three have not arrived in time
khob, in lulehâ ru-ye-lâri bogzârid	= All right, put these pipes on the lorry
shomâ chè kâr mikonid ? bar-e yek lulè hasht nafar lâzem ast ?	= What are you doing ? Do you need eight men for one pipe ?
âghâ-ye-shôfer, in lâri tâ sar-e-kuh bebarid. dah nafar hamrâh berand	= Driver, take this lorry to the top of the hill. Ten men go with it
to chè kâr mikoni ?	= What are you doing ?
khalâfam chi-è ? hich chizi nakardam	= What is wrong ? I have done nothing

râst migid, âghâ, ammâ injâ = You are right, but here you
lâzem ast yâ kâr bokonid yâ   must work or go
berid

khabar dâr ! radd shô ! un lulè = Look out ! Get out of the
miyoftad !   way ! That pipe is falling !

ânjâ chè bâzi mikonid ? ân = What are you playing at ?
lulè shâyad be-kasi zadè   That pipe might have hit
bâshad   someone

un sè tâ safhè-ye-âhan-i kè = Where are thsoe three iron
diruz az ambâr ferestâdand   plates which came from
kojâ hastand ?   the store yesterday ?

al'ân miyârim âghâ ; rezâ = We will bring them at once,
gholi, hasan ali, beyid zud   sir ; Reza Gholi and
komak bedid   Hasan Ali, come quickly
    and help

bolandesh kon, bolandesh kon ! = Lift it up, lift it up ! Can it
mishad yâ namishad ?   be done or not ?

ali jân, shoma az hamè-ye- = Ali Jan, you are the laziest
kârgerân tanbaltar-id; cherâ   of all the men ; why don't
kâratân namikonid ?   you do your work ?

chè migid, âghâ ? zur nist ; = What are you saying, sir ?
agar mêl nadâram kâr   There is no compulsion ;
bokonam, namikonam   if I don't wish to work,
    I won't

besyâr khob ; mêl-e-shomâ-st. = Very well ; as you like.
ekhrâj shodid, borô edârè   You are discharged ; go
pulatun begirid   to the office and get your
    money

âghâ, pish-e-shahrabâni   = I shall complain to the
shekâyat mikonam   police

kêf-e-khodatân. vali mesl-e- = Just as you wish. But we
shomâ injâ lâzem nadârim   don't want men like you
    here

In Camp

âghâ-ye-sar-amalè, injâ sè tâ châdor bezanid ; az ân taraf chahâr tâ lâzem ast	Foreman, pitch three tents here ; four are wanted over there
besyâr khob âghâ. ja'far o karim, zud berid az lâri haft tâ châdor bâ chubhâsh o mikhhâsh beyârid	Very good, sir. Ja'far and Karim, go quickly and bring seven tents from the lorry with poles and pegs
âghâ, mâ dô nafar hastim ; chè tor mishad haft tâ châdor beyârim ?	Sir, we are only two ; how can we bring seven tents ?
êb nadârad, dô nafar az rafighhâtân ham bebarid	Never mind, take two of your companions as well
vaghti kè châdorhâ khob zadid, har yek dôresh yek jub bekanid	When you have pitched the tents properly, dig a trench round each one
balè, âghâ. ali akbar, beyâ in chub boland kon, bâghiyetân mikhhâ-râ tu zamin bokubid	Yes, sir. Ali Akbar, come and hold this pole up, while the rest of you hammer in the pegs
in châdor mâl-e-ambâr ast. asbâbhâ-i kè tu un lâri-ye-digar pêdâ mishad beyârid o tush bezanid	This is the store tent. Bring those goods in the other lorry and put them in it
âghâ, in bokhâri tu lâri bud, hâlâ shekastè shod. bar-e-shâm chè kâr mikonim ?	Sir, this stove was in the lorry and has got broken. What shall we do for supper ?
âghâ, har chè gashtim, bilhâ pêdâ nakardim	Sir, however much we have searched, we have not found the spades
âsemân khêli gereftè ast ; fekr mikonam al'ân bârun miyâd	The sky is very cloudy ; I think it will rain directly

pas berid zud châdorhâ bezanid. = Then go and pitch the tents
cherâ injâ vâ istâdid ?   quickly. Why are you
       standing here ?

âghâ, mâ se nafar hastim, = Sir, we three don't know
asbâbamân namidânim kojâ   where our kit has gone ;
raft. shâyad az shahr   perhaps we left it in the
nayâvardim   town

janâb-e-ra'is, delam khêli tang = Sir, I am feeling very ill ;
shod ; bi zahmat yek khordè   please give me a little
davâ bedid   medicine

hâlâ hametân berid bekhâbid ; = Now all of you go to sleep,
fardâ sobh sâ'at-e-haft bar-   and be ready for work at
e-kâr hâzer bâshid   seven in the morning

âghâ, shâm hâzer shod !   = Supper is ready, sir.

alhamdo-lellâh !   be-khodâ = Thank goodness ! Good
ghasam, in gusht chè tôr   heavens, what has
shod ?   happened to this meat ?

âghâ, chè midânam ? bokhâri = How should I know, sir ?
nabud, chand tâ mikh âtesh   There was no stove, so I
zadam va ântôr dorost   made a fire of some pegs
kardam   and cooked it like that

fardâ sobh mêl dâram sevâri = To-morrow morning I want to
bokonam ; asbam-râ bâ zin   ride; have my horse ready
o yerâgh hâzer konid   with saddle and harness

âghâ, yek âzhân âmadè ast, = Sir, a policeman has come
migad injâ ejâzè nist   who says we are not
châdorhâ bezanim, lâzem ast   allowed to pitch tents
hamè chiz jam' konim o   here, and we must pack
berim   everything up and go

âghâ-ye-âzhân, fardâ sobh zud = Constable, we are moving
harakat mikonim ; ejâzè   early to-morrow morning;
namidid emshab injâ   won't you let us stay here
bemânim ?   to-night ?

VOCABULARIES

* New words not yet in general use.

n. Noun.

v. Verb.

a. Adjective.

When alternative meanings are given, one of them is generally Persian and the other Arabic.

The verbs in brackets are those usually used with the words in question, as described in Paras. 40 to 41.

In the Persian-English vocabulary the stem of the irregular verbs is given in brackets.

None of the vocabularies include words already listed in the lessons, e.g. in Lesson VIII.

A. ENGLISH-PERSIAN

1. MILITARY, NAVAL, AND AIR

about turn !	= berâst gard !	*anchorage*	= langargâh
adjutant	= mo'ayyen, âjudân	*anti-aircraft*	= zedd-havâpêmâ-i
		armament	= aslehè, taslihât
aerodrome	= mêdân-e-tay-yârè, forud-gâh*	*armed forces*	= arte<u>sh</u>,* niru-ye-nezâmi
aeroplane	= tayyârè, bâlun (colloq.), hâvâ-pêmâ*	*armistice*	= motârakè-ye-jang
		arms	= aslehè
bomber ——	= —— -ye-bomb-andâz	*port* —— *!*	= hamâyel fang !
		present ——,	= pi<u>sh</u> fang !
		sling —— *!*	= band fang !
fighter ——	= —— -ye-<u>sh</u>ekâri	*slope* —— *!*	= du<u>sh</u> fang !
air force	= niru-ye-havâ-i	*under* ——	= taht-as-sclâh
air raid	= torktâzi-ye-havâ-i	*armour-plate*	= safhè-ye-âhan
		armoured	= zarrè-pu<u>sh</u>
airship	= jahâz-e-havâ-i	*armourer*	= aslehè-sâz
allowance	= fô<u>gh</u>alâdè	*army*	= sepâh, <u>gh</u>o<u>sh</u>un, la<u>sh</u>kar
travelling ——	= <u>kh</u>arj-e-safar		
ambush	= kamingâh	*army corps*	= kordârmè
ammunition	= mohemmât	*arrest*	= habs, jolôgiri
anchor	= langar	*arsenal*	= zarrâd <u>kh</u>ânè, <u>gh</u>urk<u>h</u>ânè
to cast anchor	= —— andâ<u>kh</u>tan		

103

artillery	= tupkhânè	division	= lashkar
attack	= hamalè	dredger	= shankash*
attention !	= hâzer bâsh !	drum	= tabl
	khabar dâr !	dynamite	= dinâmit
auxiliary	= komaki	embargo	= tôghif
badge	= neshân, neshânè	embark	= sevâr shodan
barge	= karaji		(kardan)
barracks	= sarbâz-khânè	engagement	= razm*
barricade	= sangar, sadd	engine (plane,	= môtôr
base	= noghtè-ye-ettekâ	etc.)	
battalion	= gerdân	equipment	= sâzobarg
battle (naval)	= nabard*	escort	= badraghè
battle-cruiser	= nabardnâv	espionage	= jâsusi
bayonet	= sarnêzè	evacuation	= takhliyè
belligerent	= motahâreb	explode	= monfajar shodan
blockade	= mohâsarè		(kardan), tarki-
blockhouse	= sangar, ghal'è		dan
bomb	= bomb	eyes right (left) !	= nazar be-râst
bombardment	= bombârân		(chap) !
brigade	= tip	field-day	= ruz-e-sân
bullet	= golulè	fire (shot)	= tir andâkhtan
cartridge	= fashang	flag	= bêragh,
cavalry	= ghoshun-e-sevâri		parcham*
command (order)	= farmân, farmân-	flank	= pahlu
	dehi	fleet	= bahriyè,
company	= gerdân		nâvegân*
compass	= ghotbnemâ	flotilla	= nâvgoruh (= 2-
conscription	= nezâm-e-vazifè		3 dastè),
(liable for——)	= mashmul		nâvtip (= 2-3
convoy	= badraghè		nâvgoruh)
court-martial	= mahkamè (dâd-	fortification	= sangar, sadd,
	gâh)-e-nezâmi		ghal'è
crew	= amalè, jâshu	fortress	= sangar, ghal'è
cruiser	= razmnâv*	frontier	= sarhadd, marz*
armoured——	= zarrè-nâv,*	fuselage	= fuzelâzh, tanè*
	kurâsè	garrison	= sâkhlu, pâdegân*
demobilize	= monhall kardan	gas	= gâz
demobilization	= enhelâl	gas mask	= mâsk-e-zedd-gâz
deploy	= saff kashidan	G.O.C.	= sar-lashkar,
desert	= ferâr kardan		sepahsâlâr
deserter	= ferâri	grenade	= nâranjak
destroyer	= nâv-shekan*	guard	= pâdegân, pâsdâr,
dinghy	= ghâ'egh, karaji		gharâvol, post
disembark	= peyâdè shodan	guard room	= pâsgâh, gharâ-
	(kardan)		volkhânè
displacement	= zarfiyat	gun (shot)	= tofang
23,000 tons —	= be-zar-fiyat-e-	gun (artillery)	= tup
	bist-o-sè-hazâr	gunboat	= tupdâr, kânunyir
	ton	gunner	= tupchi

gunpowder	= bârut	rank (*line*)	= saff
halt !	= ist !	(*seniority*)	= rotbè, darajè
icebreaker	= ya<u>kh</u>-<u>sh</u>ekan	recruitment	= sarbâzgiri
infantry	= <u>gh</u>o<u>sh</u>un-e-peyâdè	refugee	= mohâjer, penâhandè
information intelligence }	= ettelâ'ât	regiment	= hang
		reserve	= za<u>kh</u>irè
irregular (*troops*)	= <u>kh</u>ârej az saff	revolver	= tapân<u>ch</u>è
keel	= tah(-e-ka<u>sh</u>ti)	rifle	= tofang
land (*plane*)	= forud âmadan	right (*left*) turn !	= râst (chap) gard!
land forces	= niru-ye-zamini	rower	= pâruzan
machine-gun	= tup-e-mosalsal	rowlock	= pârugir
magazine	= fa<u>sh</u>angdân	sailing boat	= koru
map	= na<u>ghsh</u>è	sailor	= malavân, bahri
mast	= dagal	section	= dastè (naval = 2 ships), ju<u>kh</u>è
military service	= <u>kh</u>edmat zir-e-par<u>ch</u>am	sentry	= negâhbân,* ka<u>sh</u>ik<u>ch</u>i
mine (*naval*)	= min	shell	= golulè, nâranjak
minesweeper	= min-jam'-kon	ship	= ka<u>sh</u>ti, jahâz
mobilization	= basij	fishing ——	= —— e-mâhi-gir
motor boat	= lân<u>sh</u>, <u>gh</u>â'e<u>gh</u>, karaji	merchant ——	= —— e-tejârati
motorized forces	= niru-ye-môtôrizè	passenger ——	= —— e-mosâferi
		steam ——	= —— e-bo<u>kh</u>âri
mounted	= sevârè	warship	= nâv, nâv<u>ch</u>è ka<u>sh</u>ti-ye-jangi
nautical	= daryâ-i, bahri		
naval forces	= niru-ye-daryâ-i	shot	= tir
navy	= nâvegân, bahriyè	sight	= did
noncombatant	= <u>gh</u>êr nezâmi	sink	= <u>gh</u>ar<u>gh</u> kardan
oar	= pâru	siren	= sut
oarsman	= pâruzan	skiff	= karaji, <u>gh</u>â'e<u>gh</u>
officer	= afsar, sâhebmansab (see separate list for ranks)	sloop	= pâygerd,* eksplôrâtur
		soldier	= sarbâz
		squadron (*naval*)	= ba<u>kh</u>s<u>h</u>,* eskadr
order	= farmân	stand at ease !	= râhat bâ<u>sh</u> !
parachute	= <u>ch</u>etr	stern	= donbâl
patrol	= ga<u>sh</u>ti, ju<u>kh</u>è, pâs*	stock (*gun*)	= <u>gh</u>anda<u>gh</u>
		submarine	= zir-daryâ-i, taht-al-bahri
pilot (*air*)	= <u>kh</u>albân,* tayyâre<u>ch</u>i		
platoon	= rasad, fôj	tail (*plane*)	= donbâlè
post (*military*)	= post	take off (*plane*)	= parvâz dâdan
prisoner	= gereftâr	tank	= tânk
prohibited (*area*)	= mamnu'(-al-vorud)	target	= hadaf
		torpedo	= e<u>zh</u>dar,* torpil
pursue	= donbâl kardan	—— boat	= e<u>zh</u>dar-afkan,* torpilur
puttee	= pâpi<u>ch</u>		
Q. M.	= kârpardâz	—— tube	= e<u>zh</u>dar-andâz,* lâns-torpil

trench	= k͟handag͟h	*unmounted*	= peyâdè
truce	= solh	*volley*	= s͟halik
tug	= kas͟hidè-karaji	*volunteer*	= dâvtalab
turret	= borj	*watch (patrol)*	= gas͟hti, pâs
under-carriage	= arrâdè	*wing*	= bâl
unit	= vâhed		

MILITARY, ETC., RANKS

Army (artes͟h)	Navy (nâvegân)	Police (s͟hahrabâni)
sarbâz *private*	nâvi *rating*	pâsbân (âz͟hân) *constable*
afsar-e-joz' *N.C.O.*	—	—
goruhbân-sè (sarjuk͟hè) L/*Corporal*	sarnâvi	sar-pâsbân-sè
goruhbân-dô *Corporal*	mehnâvi-dô	„　　„　-dô
„　　-yek *Sergeant*	„　　-yek	„　　„　-yek
ostovâr-dô *Sgt.-Major*	nâv-ostovâr-do	
„　　-yek *R.S.M.*	„　　„　-yek	—
afsar-e-ars͟had *Commissioned Officer*	—	pâyvar *officer*
setvân-sè (nâ'eb) 2nd *Lieutenant*	nâvbân-sè *Sub-Lieut.*	rasadbân-sè
setvân-dô *Lieutenant*	„　　-dô *Lieutenant*	„　　-dô
„　　-yek „	„　　-yek „	„　　-yek
sarvân (soltân) *Captain*	nâvsarvâb *Lt.-Com.*	sarbahr
sargerd (yâvar) *Major*	nâk͟hodâ-sè *Commander*	yâvar
sarhang-dô *Lieut.-Col.*	„　　-dô *Captain*	pâsyâr-dô
„　　-yek *Colonel*	„　　-yek	„　　-yek
sartip *General*	daryâdâr *Vice-Adm.*	sarpâs
sepahbod *Field-Marshal*	daryâbân *Admiral*	—
sepahsâlâr *G.O.C.*	daryâsâlâr *Admiral of the Fleet*	s͟hahrdâr

2. TECHNICAL, ETC.

alcohol	= alkol	*brass*	= berenj
aluminium	= aluminyum	*bridge*	= pol, jesr
apparatus	= dastgâh	*bridle*	= afsâr
automatic	= k͟hodkâr	*building*	= amârat
automobile	= mâs͟hin, otomobil	*camera*	= aksnâmè
drive ——	= —— rândan	*canvas*	= c͟hetri
—— *driving*	= —— râni	*carburetteur*	= suk͟htâmâ*
axe	= tabar		kârburâtur
battery	= bâtri	*carriage (railway)*	= vâgon
bicycle	= dô-c͟hark͟hè		
binoculars	= durbin	*cement*	= simân
bit	= dahanè	*chain*	= zanjir

charabanc	= shârâbân, otobus	private lorry	= —— ye-shakhsi
chemistry	= shimi	commercial ——	= —— ye-tâksi
chimney	= dudkash	machine	= makinè, mâshin-e-âlât
chisel	= eskenè		
clutch	= klâch, chang*	mallet	= mikhku(b)
cog	= kongerè, dandânè	mathematics	= reyâz
		mine (mineral)	= ma'dan, kân*
construction	= sâkhtemân	mineral (adj.)	= ma'dani
copper	= mas	motor car	= mâshin, otomobil
corrugated	= môji		
craft (trade)	= san'at	private motor car	= —— e-shakhsi
drill	= mattè		
drilling rig	= makinè	taxi	= —— e-tâksi
droshky	= doroshkè	motor cycle	= motorsiklet
—— driver	= —— chi	mould	= ghâb, ghâleb
electric light bulb	= âmpul, cherâgh-e-bargh	mudguard	= gelgir
		nail	= mikh
electricity	= bargh	needle	= suzan
employee	= kârkon, mostakhdem	omnibus	= shârâbân, otobus
		oil	= naft
employer	= arbâb, kârfarmâ	asphalt ⎫ bitumen ⎭	= âsfâlt
enamel	= minâ	crude ——	= naft-e-seyâh
engine (cars, etc.)	= môtôr	diesel ——	= naft-e-dizel
engineer (civil)	= mohandes	fuel ——	= naft-e-seyâh
factory	= kârkhânè	grease	= gris
funnel	= ghif	kerosene	= naft-e-safid
fuse (electric)	= fyuz	liquid paraffin	= parafin-e-mâye'
gear	= charkh-e-dandânè	lubricating oil	= rôghan
		paraffin wax	= mum-e-ma'dani
gimlet	= mattè	petrol	= benzin
girder	= tir(-e-âhan)	petroleum	= naft
girth	= tang	turpentine	= torbântin-e-ma'dani
groundsheet	= chetri		
gold	= talâ	vaseline	= vâzlin
hammer	= chakosh	oil fields	= ma'âden-e-naft
handle	= dastè, dastgirè	pedal	= jâ-pâ, pâ-i
harness	= setâm, yerâgh	per cent	= dar sad
horn	= bugh	percentage	= sadi
blow ⎫ sound ⎭ ——	= —— zadan	photograph	= aks
		take photograph	= ⎧ —— gereftan ⎩ —— bar dâshtan
horse-shoe	= na'l	photography	= aks bardâri, aksgiri
iron	= âhan		
ladder	= pellè	physics	= fizik
lamp	= cherâgh	pickaxe	= kolang
lead	= sorb	pipe	= lulè
lever	= ahram	pliers	= dam-pahan
locomotive	= lokomotiv	prong	= sikh
lorry	= lâri		

pump (oil, water, etc.)	= telembè	telegraph office	= —— khânè
puncture	= panchar	telephone	= telfon (kardan)
radio	= râdyô	tent	= châdor
rail points	= suzan	pitch tent	= —— zadan
railway	= râh-e-âhan, khatt-e-âhan	strike ——	= —— pa'in kar¹ dan
receiver	= dastgâh-e-râdyô	tent peg	= mikh
refinery	= tasfiyè-khânè, pâleshgâh	tin	= ghuti
		train	= ghetâr
		training	= tajrebè
reins	= zemâm	transmitter	= post-e-fere-standè
rubber	= lâstik		
saddle	= zin	transport	= naghliyè, bârkashi
sack(ing)	= guni		
saw	= arrè	triangular	= mosallas
screw	= pich	tyre	= tâyr, lâstik
screwdriver	= âchâr	valve (tyre)	= vâlv
silver	= noghrè	valve (wireless)	= lâmp
siren	= sut	wagon (railway)	= vâgon
smoke	= dud	water-channel	= ghanât
spade	= bil	wave	= môj
spike	= sikh	short wave	= —— e-kutâh
spring	= fener	long ——	= —— e-boland
spurs	= mehmiz	wheel	= charkh
square	= morabba'	whistle	= sut
stable	= tavilè	wick	= fetilè
station	= istgâh	wire	= sim
steam	= bokhâr	wireless	= bi-sim, râdyô
steel	= pulâd	wireless station	= istgâh-e-bi-sim, post-e-râdyô
stirrup	= rekâb		
telescope	= durbin	workman	= kârger, amalè
telegraph	= teleghrâf (kardan)	workshop	= kârkhânè

3. Professions, Trades, etc.

apprentice	= shâgerd	chauffeur	= shôfer
artist	= naghghâsh	clothseller	= bazzâz, pârchè-forush
artizan	= ârtizân, afsâr-mand*		
		cobbler	= kaffâsh, kafsh-duz
baker	= khabbâz, nânpaz	confectioner	= ghannâd, shirini-forush
barber	= salmâni		
blacksmith	= âhanger	coppersmith	= masger
bookseller	= ketâb-forush	craftsman	= san'atgir
bricklayer	= bannâ	doctor	= hakim, doktor
butcher	= ghassâb	driver	= shôfer
candidate	= dâvtalab	firewatchman	= âteshkâr
carpenter	= najjâr	fishmonger	= mâhi-forush
carpet seller	= ghâli-forush	fitter	= mikânik

gardener	= bâghbân	*plumber*	= sorbkâr
grocer	= baghchâl	*porter*	= hammâl
ironmonger	= âhan-forush	*sweeper*	= jârukâr
launderer	= rakht-shu	*syce*	= sâyes
mason	= bannâ	*tailor*	= khayyât
mechanic	= mikânik	*watchmaker*	= sâ'atsâz
messenger	= farrâsh	*watchman*	= tofangchi
muleteer	= chârvâdâr	*wine merchant*	= arak-forush
painter	= naghghâsh,	*wireman*	= sim-kash
	rangzan	*workman*	= kârger, amalè
peasant	= fallâhi		(*pl.* amalejât)

4. COMMERCIAL, OFFICE, ETC.

accounts	= hesâb	*director*	= modir
agency	= kârgozâri	*document*	= nâmè
assistant	= mo'âven	*drawer*	= khânè
bank	= bânk	*employment*	= estekhdâm,
bill	= hesâb		kârgazini*
blotting paper	= khoshk-kon	*envelope*	= pâket
calendar	= taghvim, ruz-	*goods*	= kâlâ
	shomâr*	*gratis*	= majjânâ
capital	= sarmâyè	*hand over*	= tahvil kardan
carbon	= karbon, barger-	*hire*	= kerâyè
	dân*	*industry*	= sanâ'at
certificate	= tasdigh, gavâhi*	*ink*	= morakkab
circular	= bakhshnâmè	*insurance*	= bimè
class (in train,	= darajè	*letter*	= kâghez, khatt
etc.)		*licence*	= javâz, parvânè*
clerk	= monshi, mirzâ	*loading note*	= bârnâmè
commerce	= tejârat, bâzar-	*loan*	= gharz (kardan,
	gâni*		dâdan)
company	= sherkat	*manager*	= ra'is
limited com-	= sherkat-e-	*general* ——	= ra'is-e-koll
pany	sehâmi	*member*	= ozv, kârmand*
contract	= kontrât, gherâr-	*memorandum*	= dast-khatt, yâd-
	dâd*		dâsht
copy	= sevâd, ru-	*news agency*	= khabargozâri
	navesht	*note*	= khatt, dast-
cupboard	= dulâb, ganjè		khatt
date	= târikh	*note book*	= daftar
debt	= vâm,* gharz	*notice*	= e'lân, âgâhi*
department	= edârè, sho'bè	*number*	= nomrè, shomârè
head of dept.	= ra'is-e-edârè	*occupation*	= kâr, shoghl, pishè
desk	= miz-e-tahrir	*office boy*	= farrâsh
diary	= taghvim, ruz-	*parcel*	= bastè
	shomâr*	*pen*	= ghalam
dictionary	= ghâmus, farhan-	*pencil*	= madâd, ghalam
	gestân	*pledge*	= rahn (gozâshtan)

printing	= châp	secretary	= dabir
printing works	= —— khânè	security	= rahn (gozâshtan)
profit	= naf'	signature	= emzâ
programme	= barnâmè, prôgrâm	stamp (seal)	= mohr
		stamp (postage)	= tambr
receipt (document)	= ghabz, rasid*	statistics	= âmâr
		stores	= anbâr, ambâr
recommendation	= pishnehâd	telegram	= telegrâf
record	= sâbeghè, pishinè*	telephone	
register	= daftar	operator	= telefonchi
representative	= namâyandè	tender	= pishnehâd
salary	= mavâjeb, hoghugh	typist	= mashin-navis
		urgent	= fôri
seal	= mohr	wages	= mavâjeb,ma'âsh, mozd, hoghugh
sealing wax	= lâk-e-mohr		
secretarial	= dabirkhânè	year book	= sâlnemâ

5. POLITICAL AND ADMINISTRATIVE

agriculture	= fallâhat, kashâvarzi*		is divided into 49 shahrestân)
ambassador	= safir-e-kabir	court	= mahkamè, dâdgâh*
anthem	= sorud		
application	= arizè, dâdkhâst*	credentials	= ostovârnâmè
acquittal	= ma'âfiyat, bakhshudegi*	crisis	= bohrân
		cross-examination	= esteshhâd (kardan), gavâhkhâhi*
attachè	= âtâshè, vâbastè*		
birth certificate	= varaghè-ye-velâdat, zâychè*		
		customs	= gomrok
boy scout	= pish-âhang	defendant	= modda'â-alêh
break out (war)	= dar gereftan	democracy	= demukrâsi
budget	= budjè	department	= sho'bè, edârè
chargè d'affaires	= dabir, kârdâr, shâzhedâfer	deputy	= vakil
		dispensary	= davâkhânè, dârukhânè*
club	= bâshgâh		
committee conference	= anjoman	dictatorship	= dektâturi
		document	= nâmè, varaghè
consul	= konsul	Duce	= pishvâ
—— -general	= sar-konsul	economic	= eghtesâdi
vice-consul	= konsulyâr	education	= tarbiyat, parvaresh, farhang, ma'âref
consulate	= konsul-khânè		
conviction	= mahkumiyat, elzâm		
		embassy	= sefârat
council	= anjoman	evidence	= shehâdat, gavâhi*
counsel (leg.)	= vakil		
counsellor	= mostashâr, râyzan*	fatherland	= vatan
		finger-print	= mohr-e-angosht
county	= shahrestân (Iran	Führer	= pishvâ
		government	= dôlat

governor	= hokumat, hokmrân		*telegraphs and telephones*	teleghrâf o telfon
—— *of province*	= ostândâr		*ministry of roads*	= —— e-râh
—— *of county*	= farmândâr		*ministry of war*	= —— e-jang
—— *of munici-pality*	= bakhshdâr		*monopoly*	= enhesâr
—— *of rural district*	= dehdâr		*municipal*	= shahrdâri,* baladiyè
headman (village)	= kadkhodâ		*municipality*	= bakhsh
hospital	= marizkhânè		*nation*	= dôlat, kashvar
hotel	= mehmânkhânè, mosâferkhânè		*national*	= melli
identity book	= sejell(-e-ahvâl), shenâsnâmè*		*nationality*	= tâbe'iyat
imperial	= shâhanshâhi		*nationals*	= atbâ'
independence	= esteghlâl		*neutrality*	= bitarafi
inspection	= taftish, bâzrasi*		*office*	= edârè
inspector	= mofattesh, bâzras*		*official* (a.)	= rasmi
international	= bên-al-melal-i		*official* (n.)	= ma'mur
judge	= ghâzi, dâdras*		*pact*	= pêmân, ta'ahhod
king	= pâdshâh		*passenger*	= mosâfer
law	= ghânun		*passport*	= pâspôrt, gozar-nâmè
leader	= pishvâ		*permit*	= javâz, parvânè*
learning	= âmuzesh, ta'lim		*plaintiff*	= modda'i
legation	= sefârat		*police (town)*	= shahrabâni,* nazmiyè
licence	= javâz, parvânè*		*police dept.*	= edârè-ye-koll-e-shahrabâni
local	= mahalli		*policeman*	= âzhân, pâsbân*
magistrate	= ghâzi, dâdras		*police station*	= kalântari
mail	= post		*political*	= seyâsi
mediation	= meyânjigiri		*politics*	= seyâsat
minister pleni-potentiary	= vazir-e-mokhtâr		*port*	= bandar
ministry	= vezârat		*post*	= post
ministry of commerce	= vezârat-e-bâzar-gâni* (tejârat)		*post office*	= postkhânè
ministry of education	= —— e-farhang* (ma'âref)		*prime minister*	= nokhostvazir
ministry of finance	= —— e-dârâ-i* (mâliyè)		*prince*	= shâhzâdè
ministry of foreign affairs	= —— e-khârejè		*prison*	= zandân, habs
ministry of industry	= —— e-pishè va honar* (sanâ'at)		*prisoner*	= zandâni, habsi
ministry of interior	= —— e-kashvar* (dâkhelè)		*province*	= ostân (Iran is divided into 10 ostâns)
ministry of justice	= —— e-dâdgas-tari* (adliyè)		*queen*	= malekè
ministry of post, =	—— e-post o		*republic*	= jomhur
			residence permit	= javâz-e-eghâmat
			rural district	= dehestân
			school	= madrasè
			semi-official	= nimrasmi
			speech	= sokhanrâni
			student	= shâgerd

sultan	= soltân	*trial*	= mahkamè, dâdrasi*
taxation	= mâliyât	*tribe*	= il
teacher	= mo'allem	*union*	= ettehâd
tourist	= jahângard	*united*	= mottahed
traveller	= mosâfer	*visa*	= vizâ, ravâdid*
treaty	= pêmânnâmè, ta'ahhodnâmè	*witness*	= shâhed, gavâh*

6. Domestic

bag	= kif, kisè	*flour*	= ârd
bath	= hammâm	*food*	= khorâk(i)
bazaar	= bâzâr	*fork*	= changal
bedclothes	= rakht-e-khâb	*fry*	= sorkh kardan
bedroom	= khâbgâh	*frying-pan*	= tâvè
beef	= gusht-e-gâv	*gravy*	= âb-e-gusht
blanket	= patu	*hair-brush*	= mâhut
boil	= jushidan, jush kardan	*honey*	= asal
		house	= manzel, khânè
boiling water	= âb-e-jush	*house-boy*	= farrâsh
bottle	= botri, shishè	*ice*	= yakh
bowl	= kâsè, jâm	*iron (flat)*	= atu
bread	= nân	*jug*	= kuzè
breakfast	= nâshtâ	*kettle*	= ketri
broom	= jâru	*key*	= kelid, meftâh
butler	= pish-khedmat	*kitchen*	= âshpazkhânè
butter	= karè	*knife*	= kârd
candle	= sham'	*lavatory*	= mostarâh
carpet	= ghâli	*linen*	= katân
chair	= sandali, sekomli	*loaf sugar*	= ghand
cheese	= panir	*lunch*	= nahâr
cloth	= pârchè	*match*	= kebrit
coal	= zeghâl	*mattress*	= doshakk
coffee	= ghahvè	*meat*	= gusht
comb	= shânè	*milk*	= shir
confectionery	= shirini	*mustard*	= kherdal
cook	= âshpaz	*mutton*	= gusht-e-gusfand
cook (to)	= pokhtan, dorost kardan	*oven*	= bokhâri
		pepper	= felfel
cooking pot	= dik	*pillow*	= bâlesh
cup	= fenjân	*pillow-case*	= rubâlesh
curtain	= pardè	*plate*	= beshghâb
dish	= zarf	*pork*	= gusht-e-khenzir
dining-room	= mizkhânè	*powder*	= pudr
dough	= khamir	*purse*	= kisè
eiderdown	= lahâf	*razor*	
face-cream	= khamir	*razor blade* }	= tigh
fat	= rôghan	*room*	= otâgh, khânè
firewood	= hizam	*rug*	= ghâlichè

salt	= namak	supper	= shâm
saucepan	= dikchè	table	= miz
saucer	= na'lbaki	table-cloth	= rumiz
scent	= etr	tea	= chây
servant	= nôkar	teapot	= ghuri
sew	= dukhtan (duz)	toilet	= tartib
shave	= tarâshidan	toothbrush	= mesvâk
sheet	= shamad, lafâf	toothpaste	= khamir-e-dandân
shop	= dokkân	towel	= hôlè
silk	= abrisham	tray	= sim
soap	= sâbun	vinegar	= sarkè
spoon	= ghâshogh	water pot	= kuzè
stove	= bokhâri	water vessel	= hob
sugar	= sheker	window	= panjarè, darichè
suitcase	= kif	wool	= pashm

7. CLOTHES

apron	= pishdâman	pocket	= jib
blouse	= pirâhan	pyjamas	= lebâs-e-khâb
boot	= putin	scarf	= dastmâl
braces	= band-shalvâr	shawl	= shâl
button	= dokmè	shirt	= pirâhan
clothes	= lebâs, rakht	shoe (Iranian)	= givè
coat	= kot	shoe (European)	= kafsh
collar	= yaghè	shoe-lace	= bandkafsh
cummerbund	= kamarband	skirt	= dâman
dress	= lebâs	socks	= jurâb
dressing-gown	= lebâs-e-shab	sock-suspenders	= bandjurâb
fashion	= mod	spectacles	= ênak
fur	= khaz	stockings	= jurâb(-e-boland)
fur-coat	= pâltô-e-pust, zhâket-e-pust	stud	= dokmè, gol
		suit	= dast-e-lebâs
gloves	= dast-kash	tie	= krâvât
handkerchief	= dastmâl	trousers	= shalvâr, pântâlun
hat	= kolâh		
nightdress	= pirâhan-e-khâb		
overall	= shalvâr-e-kâr, lebâs-e-kâr	umbrella	= chetri
		veil	= châdor
overcoat	= pâltô	waistcoat	= jalighè

8. PLANT LIFE

alfalfa	= alaf	beetroot	= choghondar
almond	= badam	cabbage	= kalam
apple	= sib	cauliflower	= kalamgol
apricot	= zardâlu	chaff	= kâh
barley	= jô	cherry	= âlubâlu, gilâs
bean	= lubyâ	cotton	= pembè

date	= khormâ	orange	= nâranj,
fig	= anjir		portoghâl
flower	= gol	peach	= holu
fruit	= mivè	pear	= golâbi
grapes	= angur	plum	= âlu
grass	= sabzè, alaf	pomegranate	= anâr
greengage	= gujè	potato	= síb-e-zaminı
greens	= sabzi	quince	= beh
hay	= kâh	radish	= torbchè
leaf	= barg	raisin	= keshmesh
lemon	= limu	rice	= berenj
lettuce	= kâhu	rose	= gol
marrow	= kadu	straw	= hasir
melon	= hendovânè,	tree	= darakht
	kharbuzè	turnip	= shalgham
mulberry	= tut	vegetables	= sabzi
mushroom	= ghârch	walnut	= gerdu
nut	= jôz, fondogh	wheat	= gandam
onion	= peyâz		

9. ANIMALS, BIRDS, FISH AND INSECTS

ass	= khar	horse	= asb
bear	= khers	hyena	= kaftar
bee	= zanbur	jackal	= shaghâl
bird	= morgh	lamb	= barrè
buffalo	= gâvmish	leopard	= palang
calf	= gusâlè	lion	= shir
camel	= shotor	lizard	= bozmajjè, mâr
cat	= ghorbè	locust	= malakh
centipede	= sadpâ	mosquito	= pashè
chicken	= morgh	mouse	= mush
crow	= kolâgh	mule	= ghâter
dog	= sag	nightingale	= bolbol
donkey	= khar	ox	= gâv
dove	= kabutar	pig	= khenzir
duck	= morghâbi	pigeon	= kabutar
elephant	= fil	quadruped	= chahârpâ
fish	= mâhi	rabbit	= khargush
fly	= magas	rat	= mush
flea	= kik	scorpion	= aghrab
fox	= rubâh	sheep	= gusfand
gazelle	= ghazal	snake	= mâr
goat	= boz	sparrow	= gonjeshk
goose	= ghâz	tiger	= babar
grouse	= khorus	vulture	= kargas
hare	= khargush	wolf	= gorg
hoopoe	= hadhad		

10. PARTS OF THE BODY

ankle	= ghuzak	*hip*	= gardè
arm	= bâzu	*jaw*	= fakk
back	= posht	*kidney*	= gholvè
blood	= khon	*knee*	= zânu
body	= tan	*leg*	= sâgh
bone	= ostokhân	*lip*	= lab
breast	= sinè	*liver*	= jagar, kabad
cheek	= gunè	*lung*	= riyè
chest	= sinè	*mouth*	= dahan
chin	= chânè	*neck*	= gardan,
ear	= gush		onogh
elbow	= âranj	*nose*	= bini, demâgh
eye	= chashm	*pulse*	= nabz
eyebrow	= âbru	*rib*	= dandè, zol'
eyelash	= mozhè	*shoulder*	= dush
eyelid	= pelk	*skin*	= pust
face	= surat, ru	*stomach*	= shekam
finger	= angosht	*thigh*	= rân
fingernail	= nâkhon	*throat*	= golu
foot	= pâ	*thumb*	= shast
gums	= lessè	*toe*	= angosht(-e-pâ)
hair	= mu	*tongue*	= zabân
hand	= dast	*tooth*	= dandân
head	= sar	*vein*	= varid
heart	= del	*waist*	= kamar
heel	= pâshnè	*wrist*	= moch

11. PROPER NAMES
(i) *Countries*

Africa	= efrighâ	*Hungary*	= majârestân
America	= amrikâ	*India*	= hendustan
Asia	= âsyâ	*Iran*	= irân
Austria	= otrish	*Persian (lan-*	= fârsi
Balkan	= jazir-e-bâlkân	*guage only)*	
Peninsula		*Iraq*	= erâgh
Belgium	= belzhik	*Irish Free State*	= dôlat-e-âzâd-e-
British Empire	= emperâturi-ye-		irland
	britânyâ	*Italy*	= itâlyâ
Bulgaria	= bolghârestân	*Japan*	= zhâpan
China	= chin	*Mongolia*	= moghul
Egypt	= mesr	*Norway*	= nurzh
England	= englestân	*Palestine*	= falastin
English	= englis	*Persian Gulf*	= khelij-e-fârs
France	= ferânsè	*Poland*	= lahestân
Germany	= almânyâ	*Romania*	= rumâni
Greece	= yunân		

Russia	= rusyâ	U.S.A.	= êtâzuni; kashvarhâ-yemottahed-e-amrikâ
Scotland	= eskâtland		
Spain	= espânyâ		
Sweden	= su'id		
Switzerland	= su'is	U.S.S.R.	= ettehâd-e-jamâhir-e-shuravi
Syria	= suryâ		
Turkey	= torkiyè		

(ii) Common Personal Names

Male

abbâs	khalil	abdolaziz	gholâm moham-
ahmad	khosrô	abdolhosên	mad
ali	loftè	abdolkarim	,, rezâ
aziz	mahdi	abdorrahim	hasan ali
bâgher	menuchehr	abolghâsem	,, âghâ
bârân	mohammad	abdollâh	,, gholi
dâ'ud	mo'men	farajollâh	hosên ali
ebrâhim	mortezâ	fathallâh	,, gholi
elyâs	moslem	habibollâh	jân mohammad
eshâgh	mostafâ	nasrollâh	khodâdâd
esmâ'il	musâ	shokrollâh	khodâ karim
faridun	nâser	yadollâh	lotf ali
fêruz	parviz		mohammad
gudarz	rahim	ali akbar	gholi
ghâsem	rezâ	,, asghar	,, rezâ
gholâm	rostam	,, gholi	,, taghi
hasan	sâlem	,, hosên	rezâ gholi
hosên	selim	,, jân	safar ali
isâ	sayyed	,, rezâ	sayyed ali
ja'far	sohrâb	cherâgh ali	,, hasan
jamshid	solêmân	gholâm abbâs	., hosên
karim	taghi	,, ali	,, moham-
kâzem		,, hosên	mad

Female

akhtar	jamilè	purân	setârè
effat	latifè	purândokht	turân
fâtemè	nâderè	ruhiyè	zênab
ghadisè	parvin	sabâ	zinat
inâ			

12. GENERAL

a, an	= yek, yeki	*bad*	= bad, kharâb
absent	= ghâyeb	*ball*	= tup
able, be	= tavânestan	*be*	= budan
above	= bâlâ	*bear (child)*	= zâdan
abuse	= fohsh (dâdan)	*beautiful*	= ghashang
accident	= hâdesè	*because*	= zirâ(kè),
accept	= ghabul kardan,		chun(kè)
	paziroftan	*because of*	= { be az }sabab-e-
accordance with, in	= banâ bar, motâbegh-e-	*become*	= shodan, gashtan, gardidan
account of, on	= az jehat-e-, bâbat-e-	*beer*	= âb-e-jô
acquainted with	= balad	*before*	= ghabl(az),
advantage	= fâyedè		pish(az)
affair	= amr (*pl.* omur)	*begin*	= shoru' kardan
after	= ba'd az, pas az	*behalf of, on*	= az taraf-e-
after(wards)	= pas, ba'd	*behaviour*	= raftâr
afternoon	= ba'd-ez-zohr	*behind*	= aghab, posht
afternoon (late)	= asr	*bell*	= zang
again	= dôbârè, dômartabè	*below*	= pâ'in, zir
		belt	= band
age	= senn	*beside*	= be-jâneb-e-
agree	= gherâr dâdan	*between*	= meyân-e-, bên
air	= havâ	*big*	= bozorg
all	= tamâm, koll, har, hamè	*bind*	= bastan
		birth(day)	= velâdat, môlud, tavallod
alone	= tanhâ		
also	= ham, nìz	*bitter*	= talkh
allow	= ejâzè dâdan	*black*	= seyâh
always	= hamishè	*blue*	= âbi
amount	= ghadr, andâzè	*book*	= ketâb
and	= va, o	*borrow*	= gharz kardan
angry	= ghazabnâk	*bottle*	= botri, shishè
answer	= javâb (dâdan)	*box*	= sandugh
anyone	= harkas	*boy*	= pesar
anywhere	= harjâ	*brackish*	= shur
arrive	= rasidan, vâred shodan	*break*	= shekastan
		bring	= âvardan, rasânidan
around	= dôr-e-		
article	= asbâb	*bring about*	= be-kâr âvardan
ask	= porsidan	—— *back*	= pas âvardan, bâz âvardan
ask (question)	= so'âl kardan		
ask for	= talab kardan, khâhesh kardan	—— *into*	= dar âvardan be-
		—— *out of*	= dar âvardan az
athletics	= varzesh	*brother*	= barâdar
attention	= eltefât	*brown*	= ghahvè-i, khâki, sorkh (reddish brown) *
pay attention	= —— namudan		
autumn	= pâ'iz		
C.P.			

bruise	= zakhm	*complete*	= tamâm
bruised, be	= zakhm khordan	*compulsion*	= zur
burn	= sukhtan	*concerning*	= râje' be-, dar
but	= ammâ, vali,		môzu'-e-
	lâken	*condition (state)*	= hâl, *pl.* ahvâl
buy	= kharidan	*condition (term)*	= shart, *pl.* sharâ-
call	= khândan, sedâ		yet
	kardan	*conduct*	= raftâr
calm	= ârâm	*corner*	= pich (*turning*);
carry away	= bordan		gushè (*angle*)
case, in any	= dar hamè hâl	*correct*	= sahih
caught, be	= gir kardan	*count*	= shomordan,
cause	= sabab		hesâb kardan
century	= gharn	*court*	= mêdân
certain	= yaghin (dâshtan)	*create*	= âfaridan
certainly	= albattè	*crimson*	= ghermez
change	= taghyir dâdan,	*crooked*	= kaj
	badal kardan,	*crown*	= tâj
	avaz kardan	*cry*	= seyâh, sedâ
cheap	= arzân		(kardan)
chess	= shatranj	*cultivation*	= zerâ'at
chief	= ra'is (*pl.* ro'asâ)	*curse*	= fohsh dâdan
child	= bachè	*custom*	= gha'edè
cigarette (smoke)	= sigâri (kashidan)	*daily*	= harruzè, ruzè
cinema	= sinemâ	*damage*	= khesârat (*n.*),
clean	= pâk (kardan)		kharâb kardan
clear away	= radd kardan		(*v.*)
cloth	= pârchè		
cloudy	= gereftè	*dance*	= raghs (*n.*), ragh-
coffee shop	= ghahvèkhânè		sidan (*v.*)
cold	= sard(a), sarmâ	*danger*	= khatar
	(*n.*)	*dangerous*	= khatarnâk
catch cold	= sarmâ khordan	*daughter*	= dokhtar
collect	= jam' kardan	*day*	= ruz
collide	= bar ham zadan	—— *after*	= pasfardâ
colour	= rang	*to-morrow*	
come	= âmadan	—— *before*	= pariruz
come (polite)	= tashrif âvardan	*yesterday*	
come back	= bâz âmadan, bar	*dead*	= mord
	gashtan	*dear*	= aziz
come into	= dar âmadan be-	*deceive*	= fereftan
come out of	= dar âmadan az	*decide*	= tasmim kardan
comfort(able)	= râhat	*decoration*	= zinat
command	= farmudan	*degree*	= darajè
companion	= hamrâh, rafigh	*demand*	= talab kardan
compatriot	= hamvatan	*desert* (n.)	= beyâbân
compelled	= majbur	*desert* (v.)	= ferâr kardan
complaint	= shekâyat	*desire*	= khâstan (*v.*),
	(kardan)		khâhesh (*n.*)
		die	= mordan

VOCABULARIES 119

die (pass away)	= fôt shodan	examination	= emtehân	
difference	= ekhtelâf, fargh	take examina-	= —— dâdan	
difficult	= moshkel, sakht	tion		
dig	= kandan	except	= joz, sevâ-ye	
direction	= taraf, dast	excessive	= zeyâd	
dirty	= kasif, nâpâk	exchange	= badal, avaz	
discharge	= ekhrâj (kardan)		(kardan)	
disinfectant	= davâ	excuse	= ozr (kardan)	
ditch	= khandagh	exert one's self	= kushesh kardan,	
division	= ghesmat		kushidan	
do	= kardan	exhibition	= namâyesh	
door	= dar	expel	= ekhrâj kardan	
down	= pâ'in	expensive	= gerân	
drag	= kashidan	expulsion	= ekhrâj	
draw	= kashidan	extinguish (light)	= khâmush kardan	
—— picture	= tasvir kashi-	extra	= foghalâdè	
	dan	fact, in	= belhaghighè,	
drink	= khordan, âshâmi-		fe'lan	
	dan, (n.) mash-	fall	= oftâdan	
	rub	—— behind	= aghab oftâdan	
drive	= rândan	family	= ayâl	
drunk	= mast	far	= dur	
dry	= khoshk	as far as	= tâ(be-)	
dust	= khâk	fast	= zud, tond	
duty	= vazifè, taklif	fasten	= bastan	
each	= har	father	= pedar	
earth	= zamin ; (soil)	fault	= êb, khalâf,taghsir	
	khâk	——, be at	= khalâf kardan,	
east (n.)	= shargh, khâvar		taghsir dâsh-	
eat	= khordan		tan, êb dâshtan	
effect	= natijè	fear	= tarsidan	
effects, personal	= asbâb, asâsiyè	festival	= id	
effort	= kushesh	few	= kam	
egg	= tokhm(-e-morgh)	fevered, be	= tab kardan	
empty	= khâli	field	= zerâ'at	
enemy	= doshman	fight	= jang, da'vâ,	
enough	= bas		mojâdalè	
entire	= tamâm	find	= pêdâ kardan,	
entrust	= sepordan		yâftan	
erect	= boland kardan	finish	= khalâss (tamâm)	
	(v.)		kardan	
escape	= ferâr kardan	finished	= khalâs	
even	= ham (adv.)	fire	= âtesh	
evening	= shab	set fire to	= —— zadan	
evenness	= hamvâri	firm	= mohkam	
every	= har	flee	= ferâr kardan	
everyone	= harkas, hamè kas	floor	= zamin	
everywhere	= harjâ, hamè jâ	fold	= tâ (kardan,	
evil-smelling	= badbu		zadan)	

for	= barâ-ye, bar-e-	*health*	= sehhat,
forbidden	= mamnu'		tandorosti
foreign	= khâreji	*be in good*	= hâl dâshtan
forget	= farâmush kar-	*health*	
	dan	*hear*	= shanidan
be forgotten	= (az)yâd raftan	*heart, by*	= bâ hefz
formerly	= sâbeghan	*learn by heart*	= hefz kardan
free	= âzâd	*heat*	= garmâ
fresh	= tâzè	*heaven*	= âsemân
friend	= dust, sadigh	*heavy*	= sangin, koloft
from	= az	*help*	= komak (dâdan)
front, in	= jolô, pish	*here*	= injâ
furniture	= asâsiyè	*high*	= boland, âli
gamble	= ghomâr kar-	*hill*	= kuh
	dan	*hole*	= surâkh ; (*pit*) gôd
game	= bâzi	*holiday*	= ta'til
garden	= bâgh	*honourable*	= sharif
rose garden	= golestân	*hope*	= omid
gate	= bâb	*hopeful*	= —— vâr
gather	= jam' kardan,	*hot*	= garm
	jam' âvardan	*hour*	= sâ'at
gentleman	= âghâ	*house*	= manzel, khânè
get	= setândan, essun-	*how ?*	= chè tôr (gunè,
	dan (coll.)		jur(è))
get up	= boland shodan	*how many ?*	= chand (tâ)
give	= dâdan	*hungry*	= gorosnè
glance	= nazar (andâkh-	*hunt*	= shekâr (kardan)
	tan)	*hurt* (intr.)	= dard kardan
glass	= shishè	(tr.)	= zakhm kardan,
go	= raftan		shekastan
—— (*polite*)	= tashrif bordan	*husband*	= shôhar
—— *back*	= bâz raftan, bar	*I*	= man
	gashtan	*idea*	= fekr
—— *out*	= birun raftan	*if*	= agar
God	= khodâ, allâh	*ill*	= nâkhosh, mariz
good	= khob, khosh, nik	*be ill*	= hâl nadâshtan
grant	= bakhshidan	*imagine*	= kheyâl kardan,
green	= sabz		tasavvor
greetings, send	= salâm dâdan		kardan
grey	= noghrè-i	*in*	= dar, dâkhel, tu
ground	= zamin	*increase*	= afzudan, ezâfè
gulf	= khelij		kardan
gun	= tofang	*inform*	= khabar dâdan
hard	= seft	*be informed*	= khabar dâshtan
(*difficult*)	= sakht	*information*	= ettelâ'ât
have	= dâshtan	*inspect*	= bâz didan,*
he	= u, in, ân		taftish kardan
head	= sar	*instead of*	= avaz-e-, badal-e-,
(*chief*)	= ra'is		bejâ-ye-

intelligence	= fahm		*life*	= zandegâni
interrupt	= ghat' kardan (namudan)		*light* (*fire*)	= âtesh zadan
			like (*similar*)	= mesl
investigate	= rasidegi kardan		*like* (v.)	= mêl dâshtan, dust dâshtan
island	= jazirè			
joke	= shôkhi (kardan)		*limit*	= hadd
journey	= safar (kardan)		*liquid*	= mâye'
just as	= chonânchè		*list*	= fehrest
keep	= negâh kardan		*listen*	= gush dâdan
kill	= koshtan		*literate, be*	= sevâd dâshtan
kind (a.)	= mehrabân		*little*	= kuchek, (*few*) kam
kind (n.)	= gunè, jur(è), tôr			
			load	= bar
kindle	= âtesh zadan		*lock* (v.)	= ghofl kardan
kindness	= eltefât, mehrabâni		*long*	= boland
			look at	= negâh kardan
kit	= asbâb		*loose*	= shol (kardan)
know (*person*)	= shenâkhtan		*lose*	= gom kardan
know (*thing*)	= dânestan		*be lost*	= gom shodan
Koran	= ghor'ân		*love*	= dust dâshtan
lady	= khânom, bânu		*lower*	= pâ'in bordan, pâ'in kardan
lame	= lang			
lane	= kuchè		*mad*	= divânè
language	= zabân		*make*	= sâkhtan
last (v.)	= tul kashidan		*man*	= mard, âdam, shakhs, nafar
last (a.)	= âkher, pasin			
last, at	= belâkherè		*manager*	= ra'is
lastly	= akhiran, âkher-e-kâr		*manliness*	= mardi
			manure	= kud, kut
late	= dir ; (*delayed*) mo'attal ; (*dead*) marhum		*many*	= besyâr, khâli
			marry	= arusi kardan
			master	= arbâb
latest	= pasin		*meaning*	= ma'nâ, ma'ni
laugh	= khandidan		*means*	= vasilè, vâsetè
lawn	= chaman		*measure*	= vazn
lay down	= nehâdan		*medicine*	= davâ
lazy	= tanbal		*memento*	= yâdkâr
learn	= âmukhtan, yâd gereftan		*method*	= tarz
			midday	= zohr
least, at	= aghallan		*middle*	= vasat
leather	= charm		*midst of, in the*	= meyân-e-
left	= châp		*mind*	= yâd
lend	= gharz dâdan		*minute*	= daghighè
lesson	= dars		*mistake*	= eshtebâh (kardan)
let go	= vel kardan			
letter (*alphabet*)	= harf		*Mr.*	= âghâ
(*correspondence*)	= kâghez, khatt		*Mrs.*	= khânom
			mix	= âmikhtan
lie (*tell*)	= dorugh (goftan)		*Mohammadan*	= moslem

Mohammadan-ism	= eslâm	*obey*	= etâ'at kardan
money	= pul	*object* (n.)	= maghsud
month	= mâh	*obliged*	= majbur
monthly	= —— eyânè	*observe*	= molâhazè kardan
moon	= mâh	*obtain*	= setândan, essundan (*coll.*)
more	= bishtar	*obtainable, be*	= gir âmadan, bedast âmadan
morning	= sobh		
Moslem	= moslem	*occur*	= vâghe' shodan
mosque	= masjed	*offer*	= ta'ârof kardan
mostly	= ghâleban	*old*	= kohnè, ghadim (*things*) ; pir (*people*)
mother	= mâdar		
mount	= sevâr kardan		
be mounted	= —— shodan	*on*	= ru, bar ru, sar, bar sar
mountain	= kuh		
mouthful	= khordè	*one*	= yek
move	= harakat kardan	*only*	= faghat, joz
much	= besyâr, khêli	*open*	= bâz, vâz (kardan)
mud	= gel	*opium*	= teryâk
murder	= ghatl	*opportunity*	= forsat (dâshtan)
naked	= lokht	*opposite*	= moghâbel(*place*), zedd (*anti-*)
name	= esm, nâm		
naturally	= tab'an	*or*	= yâ
near	= nazd, nazdik	*orange* (*colour*)	= nâranji
nearly	= taghriban	*order*	= farmudan
necessary (a.)	= lâzem	*other*	= digar, âkhar
(n.)	= lâzemè	*other than*	= ghêr az
necessaries	= lavâzem	*one another*	= yekdigar
necessary, be	= bâyestan (*impers.*)	*outside*	= birun, khârej
		owner	= sâheb
never	= hichvaght, hargez	*pain*	= dard
		suffer pain	= —— dâshtan
new	= jadid, tâzè, nô	*painful, be*	= dard kardan
news	= khabar	*paint*	= rang (zadan)
hear news	= khabar dâshtan	*pair*	= joft
newspaper	= ruznâmè	*paper*	= kâghez
nice	= ghashang	*parents*	= vâledên
night	= shab	*pass*	= gozashtan
last night	= dishab	*pass* (*mountain*)	= tang
no	= na, nakhêr, khêr	*patience*	= sabr
no, none	= hich	*pay*	= pardâkhtan, edâ kardan
noon	= zohr		
no one	= hichkas	*perhaps*	= shâyad
north	= shamâl	*permission*	= ejâzè, ezn
notice (v.)	= molâhazè kardan	*get permission*	= —— gereftan
now	= hâlâ, al'ân	*permit*	= ejâzè (ezn)dâdan
up to now	= tâ konun, tâ behâl	*person*	= shakhs, nafar, kas
number	= shomârè, nomrè	*personal*	= shakhsi

pill	= habbè	recognize	= shenâkhtan
pink	= mikhak	reckon	= hesâb kardan
place (v.)	= gozâshtan	red	= sorkh
(n.)	= jâ, makân	regard to, with	= dar khosus-e-,
plain	= mêdân		dar môzu'-e-
plant	= kâshtan	regulation	= ghâ'edè
play (v.)	= bâzi kardan	remain	= mândan
(n.)	= namâyesh	remainder	= bâghiyè
please (v.)	= pasandidan	remember	= yâd dâshtan
pole	= chub, chukh	—— (recall)	= yâd âvardan
poor	= faghir	remove	= radd kardan
position	= vaz'iyat	repair	= dorost kardan,
possible	= momken		ta'mir kardan
pour	= rikhtan	repeat	= bâz goftan
prefer	= mêl dâshtan	reply	= javâb (dâdan)
prepare	= dorost kardan	request	= talab kardan,
presence of, in	= pahlu		khâhesh kardan
the		make a request	= khâhesh kardan
present	= hâzer	require	= lâzem dâshtan
be present	= tashrif dâshtan	reserve	= negâh dâshtan
(polite)		resignation	= este'fâ
price	= ghêmat	respect of, in	= dar khosus-e-
prisoner	= dastgir	respects, pay	= salâm dâdan
private	= shakhsi	restaurant	= lughântè,
problem	= mas'alè		restôrân, meh-
prohibited	= mamnu'		mânkhânè
promise	= ghôl (dâdan)	result	= natijè
property	= mâl	return	= bar gashtan, bâz
pull	= kashidan		raftan (âma-
pure	= khâles		dan)
purple	= arghavâni	ride	= sevâr kardan
purpose	= maghsud	right (n.)	= haghgh (dâshtan)
put on (clothes)	= pushidan	(a.)	= dorost, sahih,
put out	= birun kardan		râst
quarrel	= da'vâ (jang,	—— (direction)	= râst
	mojâdalè)	ring	= zang zadan
	kardan	rise	= bar khâstan
quick	= zud, tond	river	= rud (khânè)
quiet	= ârâm	road	= râh
rain	= bârân	high road	= jâddè
raise	= boland kardan	roof	= bâm
rank	= darajè	room	= otâgh, khânè
rattle	= takân kardan	rope	= tanâb
read	= khândan	rough	= zebr
ready	= hâzer	round	= gerd
really	= belhaghighè,	rule	= ghâ'edè
	fe'lan	run	= davidan
receive	= paziroftan,	run away	= ferâr kardan
	ghabul kardan	same	= hamin, hamân

sand	= shan	soft	= narm
say	= goftan	someone	= folânshakhs
second (time)	= sâniyè	son	= pesar
secret	= serr	sorry	= mota'assef
section	= ghesmat	sort	= jur(è), gunè, tôr
see	= didan	soul	= jân
seed	= tokhm	sound (n.)	= sedâ
seek	= jostan	sound (horn)	= bugh zadan
self	= khod	south	= jonub
sell	= forukhtan	speak	= harf zadan
send	= ferestâdan	spectacle	= tamâshâ, namâ- yesh
—— for	= talabidan		
—— for (polite)	= salâm dâdan	spite of, in	= bâ vojud-e-, bâ
sense	= fahm	split	= shekâftan
service	= khedmat, vazifè	spoil	= kharâb kardan
set out	= harakat kardan	spring	= (season) behâr
shame	= khejâlat	—— (water)	= chashmè
shell (egg, etc.)	= pust	square (in town)	= mêdân
short	= kutâh	stage	= darajè
shout	= seyâh, sedâ (kardan)	stain	= lak
		stairs	= pellè
show	= neshân dâdan, namudan	stand	= istâdan
		star	= setârè
shut (v.)	= bastan	start	= harakat kardan
(a.)	= band	state	= hâl
side	= jâneb	statue	= mojassamè
at the side of	= be-jâneb-e, pahlu-ye-	status	= vaz'iyat
		steps	= pellè
silent	= khâmush	stick	= chub
since	= chun	still (adv.)	= hanuz
sincere	= khâles	still (a.)	= ârâm
sister	= khâhar	stone	= sang
sit	= neshastan	straight	= dorost, râst
skill	= honar	strait	= tangè
skilled	= honarmand	strange	= gharib
skilled in	= balad	stream	= jub
sky	= âsemân	street	= kheyâbân
sleep (n.)	= khâb; (v.) khâbidan	strike	= kuftan, zadan
		string	= rismân
go to sleep	= khâb raftan	strip	= lokht kardan
slow	= kond	strong	= ghavi, mohkam (firm)
slowly	= âhestè, yavâsh		
small	= kuchek	stuck, be	= gir kardan
small change	= pul-e-khordè, pul-e-seyâh	stupid	= nâdân, bifahm, nâfahm
smell	= bu	subject	= môzu'
smile	= khandidan	successful	= kâmyâb
smooth	= sâf (kardan)	such	= chonin, chonân
snow	= barf	suddenly	= nâgahân

summer	= tâbestân	*time*	= bâr, bârè, daf'è,
sun	= âftâb		martabè, vaght
suppose	= kheyâl kardan,	*tired*	= khastè
	gamân bordan	*to*	= be
surprise	= ajab, ta'ajjob	*to-day*	= emruz
be surprised	= ta'ajjob kardan	*together*	= hamrâh, bâham
sweet	= shirin	*to-morrow*	= fardâ, sobh
sweet smelling	= khoshbu	*to-night*	= emshab
swim	= shenâ kardan,	*too much*	= zeyâd
	dast-e-shenâ	*tools*	= asbâb
	dâshtan	*town*	= shahr
switch off (light)	= khâmush kar-	*traffic*	= naghliyè,
	dan		âmadoraft
switch on (light)	= rôshan kardan	*travel*	= safar (kardan)
system	= tarz	*trouble*	= zahmat
take	= gereftan	*take* ⸺	= ⸺ kashidan
take away	= bordan	*make* ⸺	= zeyâd kardan
⸺ *place*	= vâghe' shodan	*true*	= râst, sahih
⸺ *time*	= tul kashidan	*truth*	= haghgh (dâshtan)
tear (up)	= pârè kardan		râsti
teashop	= châykhânè	*in* ⸺	= belhaghighè,
temporarily	= movaghghatan		fe'lan
term	= shart	*try*	= kushesh kardan,
thankful ⸻⸗	⸗= mamnun, mota-		kushidan, sa'y
thank you ⸻	shakker		kardan
that (demonstr.)	= ân	*turn (round)*	= gardidan,
that (conj.)	= kè		gashtan
that is (to say)	= ya'ni	*twist*	= pichidan
theatre	= teyâtr, namâ-	*under*	= zir
	yeshgâh	*understand*	= fahmidan, mol-
theft	= dozdi		tafet shodan
then	= pas	*unemployed*	= bikâr
there	= ânjâ	*unfortunately*	= mota'assefânè
these	= inhâ	*unit*	= tâ, vâhed
they	= ishân	*united, be (of*	= joft shodan
thick	= koloft	*two)*	
thief	= dozd	*until*	
thin	= bârik	*use*	= tâ
thing	= chiz		= este'mâl, este-
think	= fekr kardan,		fâdè (kardan).
	gamân bordan		fâyedè (value)
thirsty	= teshnè	*valley*	= tang
this	= in, inak	*value*	= fâyedè
this year	= emsâl	*village*	= deh, âbâdi
those	= ânhâ	*visit*	= zeyârat
thought	= fekr, gamân	*voice*	= sôt, âvâz
throw	= andâkhtan	*voyage*	= safar (kardan)
throw out	= birun kardan	*wait*	= sabr kardan, vâ
tight	= tang		istâdan, negâh
			dâshtan

waken	= bidâr kardan	*wife*	= ayâl, zan
walk, go for a	= gardesh kardan	*wind*	= bâd
wall	= divâr	*wind* (v.)	= pichidan
want	= khâstan	*wine*	= sharâb
warm	= garm	*winter*	= zamestân
warmth	= garmâ	*wish* (v.)	= khâstan
wash	= shustan	*wish* (n.)	= khâhesh
watch (v.)	= negâh kardan	*with*	= bâ, be
watch (n.)	= sâ'at	*without*	= bi, bedun
water	= âb	*woman*	= zan
we	= mâ	*wood*	= chub, chukh
wear	= pushidan	*word*	= harf, loghat,
weary	= khastè		sokhan, vâzhè*
weather	= havâ	*work*	= kâr, shoghl
week	= haftè	*world*	= jahân, donyâ
weight	= vazn	*wound*	= zakhm
west (n.)	= gharb, bakhtar	*wounded, be*	= zakhm khordan
wet	= tar	*write*	= naveshtan
what	= chè, chi	*year*	= sâl
whatever	= harchè	—— *ly*	= —— eyânè
when	= kê	*last* ——	= pârsâl
where	= kojâ, ku	*yellow*	= zard
which	= kodâm	*yes*	= arrè
white	= safid	*yesterday*	= diruz
who	= ki	*yet*	= hanuz
why	= cherâ	*you*	= tô, shomâ

B. PERSIAN-ENGLISH VOCABULARY

aghallan	= at least	âhan	= iron
aghrab	= scorpion	âhestè	= slowly
ajab	= surprise	âkhar	= other
aks	= photograph	âkher	= last
akhiran	= lastly	âlât	= tools
alaf	= alfalfa, grass	âli	= high
al'ân	= now	âllâh	= God
albattè	= certainly	âlu	= plum
amalè (pl. amalejât)	= workman	âmadân	= come
		âmikhtan (âmiz)	= mix
amaliyât	= operations	âmukhtan (âmuz)	= learn
amârat	= building		
amir (pl. omarâ)	= prince, commander	ârâm	= quiet, still
		ârd	= flour
amniyè	= country police	âsemân	= sky, heaven
amr (pl. omur)	= affair	âshpaz	= cook
anbâr	= store	âtesh	= fire
andâkhtan (andâz)	= throw	âvardan	= bring
		âvâz	= voice, song
aragh	= drink distilled from date-palm	âzâd	= free
		bachè	= child
arbâb	= master, employer	bad	= bad
arizè	= petition, application	badal	= exchange
		baghghâl	= grocer
arrè	= saw	bahri	= naval, nautical
arrè	= yes	bakhsh	= municipality; squadron
artesh	= armed forces		
arusi	= wedding	bakhshidan	= grant
arz	= petition	balad	= skilled in, acquainted with
arzân	= cheap		
asâsiyè	= furniture	band	= shut; belt
asb	= horse	bandar (pl. banâder)	= port
asbâb	= tool, kit, article, personal effects		
		bandè	= slave (polite for " I ")
asr	= late afternoon		
avaz	= instead of; change	bannâ	= builder, mason
		barâdar	= brother
ayâl	= family, wife	barf	= snow
aziz	= dear	barg	= leaf
âb	= water	bargh	= lightning, electricity
âbâdi	= inhabited place		
âbi	= blue	bas	= enough
âbru	= eyebrow	bastan (band)	= bind, fasten
âdam	= man	bastè	= parcel
âftâb	= sun	bâb	= gate
âftâbi	= ewer (for toilet)	bâd	= wind
âghâ	= Mr., gentleman	bâgh	= garden

bâghiyè	= remainder	chub, chukh	= wood
bâham	= together	daf'è	= time, moment
bâlâ	= above	daftar	= register, note-book, file
bâlesh	= pillow		
bâr	= load	daghighè, (pl. daghâyegh)	= minute
bâr, bârè	= time		
bârân	= rain	dahanè	= bit
bâz	= back, open	dahân	= mouth
—— didan	= inspect	dandân	= tooth
—— kardan	= open	dandè	= rib
bâzâr	= bazaar	dar	= in ; door
bâzi	= game	darajè	= degree, stage
behâr	= spring (season)	darakht	= tree
berenj	= rice	dard	= pain
berenj	= brass	darichè	= window
besyâr	= many, much	dars	= lesson
beshghâb	= plate	dast	= hand
beyâbân	= desert	dastè	= handle ; section (mil.)
bên-al-melal·i	= international		
bêragh	= flag	dastgâh	= apparatus
bidâr	= awake	dastkash	= glove
bil	= spade	dastmâl	= handkerchief
birun	= outside	davâ	= medicine
bishtar	= more	da'vâ	= fight, quarrel
bokhâr	= steam	davidan	= run
bokhâri	= stove, oven	dâdan (deh)	= give
boland	= long, tall	dâkhel	= inside
bolbol	= nightingale	dânestan (dân)	= know
bordan (bar)	= carry (away)	dâshtan (dâr)	= have
borj	= tower, castle	(bar) ——	= take (photograph)
botri	= bottle	deh	= village
bozorg	= big	del	= heart
bu	= smell	demâgh	= nose
bugh	= horn	didan (bin)	= see
chakosh	= hammer	dik	= pot
chaman	= lawn	dir	= late
changal	= fork	diruz	= yesterday
chap	= left	dishab	= last night
charkh	= wheel	divânè	= mad
charm	= leather	divâr	= wall
chashm	= eye	dokhân	= smoke
chashmè	= spring (water)	dokhtar	= daughter
châdor	= tent	dokkân (pl. dakâkin)	= shop
châp	= printing		
chây	= tea	dokmè	= button
cherâgh	= lamp	donbâl	= tail
chetri	= canvas, ground-sheet, umbrella	donyâ	= world
		doroshkè	= two-wheeled horse-carriage
chiz	= thing		

dorost	= right, correct	fallâhat	= agriculture
doru<u>gh</u>	= lie	farâmu<u>sh</u>	= forgetting
do<u>sh</u>man	= enemy	fardâ	= to-morrow
dozd	= thief [nation	far<u>gh</u>	= difference
dôlat (pl. doval)	= government,	farmân	= order
dôr	= round (prep.)	farmudan	= command (v.)
dô<u>sh</u>akk	= mattress	(farmâ)	
dud	= smoke	farrâ<u>sh</u>	= messenger
du<u>gh</u>	= sour milk	fa<u>sh</u>ang	= cartridge
du<u>kh</u>tan (duz)	= sew	fâyedè	= use, advantage
dulâb	= cupboard	fehrest	= list
durbin	= telescope	fekr	= thought
du<u>sh</u>	= shoulder	fe'lan	= in fact, actually
dust	= friend	felfel	= pepper
edâ	= payment	fener	= spring (metal)
edârè	= office	fenjân	= cup
eghâmat	= residence	ferâr	= flight, escape
eghtesâd	= economics	ferestâdan	= send
ejâzè	= permission	(ferest)	
ekhrâj	= expulsion	fetilè	= wick
ekhtelâf	= difference	fil	= elephant
ekhteyâr	= choice	foh<u>sh</u>	= abuse
e'lân	= notice	folân	= so and so
eltefât	= attention	forsat	= opportunity
emâm	= religious leader	foru<u>kh</u>tan	= sell
emâmzâdè	= shrine	(foru<u>sh</u>)	
emruz	= to-day	fô<u>gh</u>alâdè	= extra
emsâl	= this year	fôri	= urgent
em<u>sh</u>ab	= to-night	fôt <u>sh</u>odan	= pass away
emtehân	= examination	gamân	= idea
emzâ	= signature	gandam	= wheat
esm	= name	gardidan	= turn, become
este'fâ	= resignation	garm	= hot
estefâdè	= use	garmâ	= heat
este<u>kh</u>dâm	= employment	ga<u>sh</u>tan (gard)	= turn, become
este'mâl	= use	bar ——	= return
e<u>sh</u>tebâh	= mistake	gaz	= kind of nougat
etâ'at	= obedience	gâh (as suffix)	= place
ettekâ	= support	gâv	= ox
ettelâ'ât	= information	gâvmi<u>sh</u>	= buffalo
ezn	= permission	gel	= mud
ez<u>h</u>dar	= mythical dragon,	gelim	= woven rug
	torpedo	gerân	= expensive
êb	= fault	gerd	= round (a.)
fag<u>h</u>at	= only	gereftan (gir)	= take
fag<u>h</u>ir	= poor	gir âmadan	= be available
fahm	= sense, under-	—— kardan	= be stuck
	standing	givè	= Iranian shoe
fahmidan	= understand	goftan (gu)	= say

gol	= rose, flower	ghâyeb	= absent
golâbi	= pear	ghâz	= goose
golulè	= bullet	gherâr	= agreement
gom	= lost	ghermez	= crimson
gomrok	= customs	ghesmat	= division, section
gorosnè	= hungry	ghetâr	= train
gozashtan (gozar)	= pass	ghêmat	= price
gozâshtan (gozâr)	= place	ghif	= funnel
		ghofl	= lock
gôd	= hole	ghomâr	= gamblin˜
gunè	= sort, kind	ghorbè	= cat
gunè	= cheek	ghotb	= axis, pole
guni	= sack(ing)	ghôl	= promise
gusfand	= sheep	ghuri	= teapot
gush	= ear	ghuti	= tin
gushè	= corner	habs	= prison
gusht	= meat	hadaf (pl. ahdâf)	= target, aim
ghabul	= acceptance	hadd (pl. hodud)	= limit
ghabz	= receipt	hadhad	= hoopoe
ghadim	= old (things)	haftè	= week
ghadr	= amount	haghgh (pl. hoghugh)	= right, due
ghahvè	= coffee		
ghalam	= pen, pencil	hakim	= doctor
ghal'è	= castle, fort	hamâyel	= sloping
ghanât	= channel	hammâl	= porter
ghand	= loaf sugar	hammâm	= bath
gharb	= west	hamrâh	= together ; companion
ghargh	= drowning	harakat	= movement
gharib	= strange	harâm	= unlawful
gharz	= loan	harf	= word, letter
ghasam	= oath	hasir	= straw
ghassâb	= butcher	havâ	= air, weather
ghashang	= pretty, nice	havâpêmâ	= aeroplane
ghat'	= cutting	hâdesè	= accident
ghatl	= murder	hâfez	= keeper
ghavi	= strong	hâl (pl. ahvâl)	= condition, state
ghazabnâk	= angry	hâzer	= present, ready
ghazâl	= gazelle	hefz	= preservation
ghâ'edè	= rule, custom	hendovânè	= melon
ghâli	= carpet	hesâb	= reckoning
ghâmus	= dictionary	hizam	= firewood
ghânun (pl. ghavânin)	= law	hob	= vessel for storing and cooling water
ghârch	= mushroom		
ghâsed	= bound for, aimed at	hokumat	= government
		honar	= skill
ghâshogh	= spoon	hôlè	= towel
ghâter	= mule	id	= festival

îl	= tribe	kâr	= work
istâdan (ist)	= stand	kârd	= knife
istgâh	= station	kâshtan (kâr)	= plant
jadid	= new	kebrit	= match
jahân	= world	kelid	= key
jahâz	= ship	kerâyè	= hire
jam'	= collection	ketâb	= book
jang	= fight, war	ketri	= kettle
javâb	= answer	kêf	= manner
javâz	= licence	kif	= suitcase
jazirè (pl. jazâyer)	= island	kisè	= purse
		kohnè	= old (things)
jâ	= place	kolâh	= hat
jâddè	= high road	koll	= all, whole
jân	= soul	koloft	= thick
jâneb	= side	kond	= slow
jâru	= broom	kongerè	= cog
jâsus	= spy	konun	= at present
jehat	= side, direction	koshtan	= kill
jesr	= bridge	kuchè	= lane
jib	= pocket	kuchek	= small
joft	= pair	kud	= manure
jonub	= south	kuftan (kub)	= strike
jostan (ju)	= seek	kuh	= mountain
joz	= except	kushidan	= try
jô	= barley	kutâh	= short
jub	= ditch	kuzè	= water pot
jukhè	= section (mil.)	khabar (pl. akhbâr)	= news
jur(è)	= kind, sort		
jurâb	= sock	khalâf	= fault
jushidan	= boil	khalâs	= finished
kabâb	= roasted cubes of meat	khamir	= paste
		khandagh	= trench
kabir (pl. kebâr)	= great	khandidan	= smile
kadkhodâ	= village headman	khar	= ass
kafsh	= shoe	kharâb	= bad
kaj	= crooked	kharidan	= buy
kalântari	= police station	kharj	= expenses
kamar	= waist	khastè	= tired
kandan	= dig	khatar	= danger
kardan	= do	khatt	= line
karè	= butter	khayyât	= tailor
kas	= person	khâb	= sleep (n.)
kasif	= dirty	khâbidan	= sleep (v.)
kashidan	= draw	khâhar	= sister
kashvar	= nation	khâk	= earth, dust
kâghez	= paper	khâles	= pure, sincere
kâh	= chaff	khâli	= empty
kâmyâb	= successful	khâmush	= silent

khândan	= call, read	mamnun	= thankful
khâne (pl. khânejât)	= house (esp. as suffix)	ma'mur	= official (n.)
		ma'ni	= meaning
khânom	= Mrs., lady	manzel	= house
khârej	= outside	mard	= man
khâstan (khâh)	= wish	marhamat	= respect
khâstan (khiz)	= rise	marhum	= respected, late (dead)
khedmat	= service		
khejâlat	= shame	mariz	= ill
khelij	= gulf	martabè	= time, moment
khesârat	= damage	mas'alè	= question, problem
kheyâbân	= street		
kheyâl	= idea	masjed (pl. masâjed)	= mosque
khêr	= no ; well		
khob	= good	mast	= drunk
khod	= self	mast	= thickened sour milk
khodâ	= God		
khon	= blood	mashmul	= conscripted
khorâk	= food	mashrub	= drink
khordan	= eat	mavâjeb	= wages
khordè	= mouthful	mâdar	= mother
khormâ	= date	mâh	= month ; moon
khosus	= concern, affair	mâhi	= fish
khosh	= good	mâl	= property, money
khoshk	= dry	mâliyât	= taxation
lafâf	= sheet	mândan	= remain
lahâf	= quilt	mâr	= snake
lang	= lame	nâshin	= motor, car
langar	= anchor	mâye'	= liquid
lashkar	= army, division	meftâh	= key
lâzem	= necessary	mehmân	= guest
lebâs	= clothes	mehrabân	= kind, gentle
lokht	= naked	melli	= national
lughântè	= restaurant	mesl	= like, similar
lulè	= pipe	mêdân	= plain, open space
ma'âref	= education	mêl	= preference
ma'âsh	= wages	mikh	= nail, peg
madâd	= pencil	mirzâ	= clerk
ma'dan (pl. ma'âden)	= mine	mivè (pl. mivejât)	= fruit
madrasè	= school	miz	= table
magas	= fly	mo'allem	= teacher
maghsud	= object	mo'attal	= late, delayed
majbur	= compelled	mo'âven	= assistant
makân	= place	modir	= director
makinè	= machine, drilling rig	mofattesh	= inspector
		moghâbel	= opposite
malakh	= locust	mohandes (pl. mohandesin)	= engineer, surveyor
mamnu'	= prohibited		

mohkam	= strong	nân	= bread
mohr	= seal, stamp	nâshtâ	= breakfast
mojâdalè	= quarrel	nâv	= ship
mokhtâr	= chosen	negâh	= look
molâhazè	= notice, attention	nehâr	= lunch
		nesf	= half
moltafet	= attentive	neshastan	= sit
momken	= possible	(neshin)	
monshi	= clerk	neshân	= showing
morakkab	= ink	nezâm	= organization
morakhkhas	= on leave, dismissed	nim	= half
		niru	= force
mord	= dead	niz	= also
mordan (mir)	= die	noghrè	= silver
morgh	= bird, chicken	noghtè	= point
mosalsal	= linked	nomrè	= number
mosâfer	= traveller	nô	= new
mostakhdem	= employee	nôkar	= servant
mostarâh	= w.c.	oftâdan	= fall
moshkel	= difficult	omid	= hope
mota'assef	= sorry	onogh	= neck
motashakker	= thankful	ostokhân	= bone
motâbegh	= in accordance with	ostovân	= cylinder, glass cup
movaghghat	= temporary	otâgh	= room
mozd	= wages	ozr	= excuse
môj	= wave	ozv (pl. a'zâ)	= member
môlud	= birth	pahlu	= flank
môzu'	= subject	panir	= cheese
mu	= hair	panjarè	= window
mum	= wax	parcham	= flag
mush	= mouse	pardâkhtan	= pay
nafar	= person	(pardâz)	
naft	= oil	pardè	= curtain
naghghâsh	= painter	pariruz	= day before yesterday
naghshè	= plan, drawing		
najjâr	= carpenter	pasandidan	= please (v.)
na'l	= horse-shoe	pasin	= latest, last
namak	= salt	pashè	= mosquito
namudan	= show	patu	= blanket
(namâ)		paziroftan	= accept
narm	= soft	(pazir)	
naveshtan	= write	pâ	= foot
(navis)		pâ'in	= down, at the foot of
nazar	= glance		
nazmiyè	= police	pâ'iz	= autumn
nâgahân	= suddenly	pâk	= clean
nâm	= name	pâket	= envelope
nâmè	= document	pâlto	= overcoat

pârchè	= cloth	râst	= right (true), right (direction), straight
pârè	= tear		
pârsâl	= last year		
pâru	= oar	rekâb	= stirrup
pâs	= guard	rikhtan (riz)	= pour
pedar	= father	rismân	= string
pelâo	= dish of rice, vegetables, chopped meat, etc.	rotbè	= rank, degree
		rôghan	= fat, lubricating oil
		rôshan	= light
pellè	= ladder, steps	ru	= face ; on
pembè	= cotton	rud (khânè)	= river
pesar	= son, boy	ruz	= day
peyâz	= onion	ruznâmè	= newspaper
pêdâ	= discovery	sabab (pl. asbâb)	= cause
pich	= screw, turning		
pichidan	= twist, wind	sabr	= patience
pir	= old (person)	sabz	= green
pirâhan	= shirt	sadd	= barrier
pishkhedmat	= butler	sadigh	= friend
pokhtan	= cook	safar	= journey
pol	= bridge	saff (pl. sofuf)	= rank, line
porsidan	= ask	safir (pl. sofarâ)	= ambassador
post	= mail ; post, guard	safhè	= sheet (paper, metal)
posht	= back ; behind, after	safid	= white
		sag	= dog
pul	= money	sahih	= true, correct
pulad	= steel	sakht	= hard, difficult
pust	= skin, shell	salâm	= peace
pustin	= fur cloak	salmâni	= barber
pushidan	= put on, wear	san'at	= craft
putin	= boot	sanâ'at	= industry
radd	= returning	sandali	= chair
rafigh	= companion	sandugh (pl. sanâdigh)	= box
raftan (rav)	= go		
raftâr	= behaviour	sang	= stone
raghs	= dance	sangin	= heavy
rahn	= pledge	sar	= head
ra'is (pl. ro'asâ)	= chief	sarbâz	= soldier
rakht	= clothes	sard	= cold (a.)
rang	= colour, paint	sardâb	= underground room used in summer
rasidan	= arrive		
rasidegi	= investigation		
rasmi	= official	sarhadd	= frontier
râh	= road	sarkâr	= master (in titles)
râhat	= comfort(able)	sarmâ	= cold (n.)
râje'	= concerning	sa'y	= attempt
rândan	= drive	sâ'at	= hour, watch

sâbe<u>gh</u>	= *former*	<u>sh</u>anidan	= *hear*
sâf	= *smooth*	(<u>sh</u>anav)	
sâ<u>gh</u>	= *leg*	<u>sh</u>arâb	= *wine*
sâheb (*pl.*	= *owner*	<u>sh</u>ar<u>gh</u>	= *east*
ashâb)		<u>sh</u>arif	= *noble*
sâ<u>kh</u>tan (sâz)	= *make*	<u>sh</u>art (*pl.*	= *condition, term*
sâl	= *year*	<u>sh</u>arâyet)	
sân	= *inspection (milit.)*	<u>sh</u>ast	= *thumb*
sâyes	= *syce*	<u>sh</u>âd	= *happy*
sefârat	= *embassy*	<u>sh</u>â'er (*pl.*	= *poet*
seft	= *hard*	<u>sh</u>o'arâ)	[*apprentice*
sehâm	= *share*	<u>sh</u>âgerd	= *student,*
sejell	= *seal, certificate*	<u>sh</u>âhed (*pl.*	= *witness*
sekomli	= *chair*	<u>sh</u>ohadâ)	
senn	= *age*	<u>sh</u>âm	= *supper*
sepah	= *army*	<u>sh</u>ehâdat	= *evidence*
sepordan (sepâr)	= *entrust*	<u>sh</u>ekam	= *stomach*
serr (*pl.* asrâr)	= *secret*	<u>sh</u>ekastan	= *break*
setândan	= *obtain*	(<u>sh</u>ekan)	
setârè	= *star*	<u>sh</u>ekâr	= *hunt*
sevâd	= *writing, copy*	<u>sh</u>ekâyat	= *complaint*
sevâr	= *mounted*	<u>sh</u>eker	= *sugar*
seyâh	= *black*	<u>sh</u>enâ	= *swimming*
seyâh	= *scream, shout*	<u>sh</u>enâ<u>kh</u>tan	= *know, recognize*
seyâsat	= *politics*	(<u>sh</u>enâs)	
sib	= *apple*	<u>sh</u>erkat	= *company*
sigâri	= *cigarette*	<u>sh</u>ir	= *lion*
sim	= *wire*	<u>sh</u>ir	= *milk*
sinè	= *chest, breast*	<u>sh</u>irin	= *sweet*
so'âl	= *question*	<u>sh</u>i<u>sh</u>è	= *glass*
sobh	= *morning*	<u>sh</u>o'bè	= *class, department*
so<u>kh</u>an	= *word*	<u>sh</u>o<u>gh</u>l	= *work, occupation*
sor<u>kh</u>	= *red*	<u>sh</u>ol	= *loose*
sôt	= *voice*	<u>sh</u>omârè	= *number*
su<u>kh</u>tan (suz)	= *burn*	<u>sh</u>omordan	= *count*
surat	= *face*	(<u>sh</u>omâr)	
surâ<u>kh</u>	= *hole*	<u>sh</u>oru'	= *beginning*
sut	= *whistle, siren*	<u>sh</u>otor	= *camel*
suzan	= *needle*	<u>sh</u>ôhar	= *husband*
<u>sh</u>ab	= *night, evening*	<u>sh</u>ô<u>kh</u>i	= *joke*
<u>sh</u>ahr	= *town*	<u>sh</u>ur	= *brackish*
<u>sh</u>ahrabâni	= *police*	<u>sh</u>ustan (<u>sh</u>u)	= *wash*
<u>sh</u>a<u>kh</u>s (*pl.*	= *person*	ta'ajjob	= *surprise*
a<u>sh</u><u>kh</u>âs)		ta'ârof	= *offer*
<u>sh</u>alvâr	= *trousers*	tab	= *fever*
<u>sh</u>am'	= *candle*	tab'an	= *naturally*
<u>sh</u>amad	= *sheet*	tabestân	= *summer*
<u>sh</u>amâl	= *north*	taft<u>ish</u>	= *inspection*
<u>sh</u>an	= *sand*	ta<u>gh</u>riban	= *nearly*

taghsir	= fault	tokhm	= seed, egg
taghyir	= change	tond	= swift
tahrir	= writing	tôr	= kind, sort
tahvil	= transference	tul	= length
tajrebè	= training, experience	tup	= ball, gun
		vaght (pl. ôghât)	= time
takân	= rattle	vakil	= deputy, sergeant
taklif	= duty		
talab	= request, demand	varaghè	= document
talkh	= bitter	varzesh	= athletics
tamâm	= entire, complete	vasat	= middle
tamâshâ	= sightseeing	vasilè (pl. vasâyel)	= means
tambr	= postage stamp		
ta'mir	= repair	vatan	= fatherland
tamyiz	= arrangement, decoration	vazifè	= duty
		vazir (pl. vozarâ)	= minister
tan	= body		
tanâb	= rope	vaz'iyat	= position, status
tanbal	= lazy	vazn	= weight, measure
tang	= narrow; girth; pass, valley	vâ istâdan	= wait
		vâghe'	= falling
tar	= wet	vâhed	= unit
taraf (pl. atrâf)	= side, direction	vâled	= parent
tarâshidan	= shave	vâred	= arriving
tarsidan	= fear	vâsetè (pl. vasâyet)	= means
tartib	= toilet		
tarz	= method	vel kardan	= let go, put down
tasavvor	= imagination	velâdat	= birth
tasdigh	= certificate	velâyat	= country, province
tasfiyè	= refining		
taslim	= surrender	vojud	= finding
tasmim	= decision	yaghin	= certain
tasvir	= drawing	yakh	= ice
tashrif	= honour	yavâsh	= slowly
ta'til	= holiday	yâd	= mind
tavallod	= birth	yâftan (yâb)	= find
tavânestan (tavân)	= be able	yâr	= friend
		zabân	= tongue; language
tavilè	= stable		
tayyârè	= aeroplane	zadan (zan)	= strike
tâ	= fold, unit	zahmat	= trouble
târikh	= date	zakhm	= bruise, wound
tâzè	= new, fresh	zamestân	= winter
tejârat	= commerce	zamin	= ground, earth
telembè	= pump	zan	= woman
teryâk	= opium	zanbur	= bee
teshnè	= thirsty	zandân	= prison
tir	= bar; arrow, shot	zandè	= alive
tofang	= gun	zandegâni	= life

zang	= *bell*	zerâ'at	= *cultivation, field*
zanjir	= *chain*	zeyâd	= *too much,*
zard	= *yellow*		*excessive*
zarf	= *dish*	zeyârat	= *visit*
zarfiyat	= *capacity*	zin	= *saddle*
zarrè	= *armour*	zinat	= *decoration*
zâdan (zâ)	= *bear (child)*	zohr	= *noon*
zebr	= *rough*	zud	= *quick, early*
zedd	= *anti-*	zur	= *compulsion*
zeghâl	= *coal*	zurkhânè	= *public gymnasium*
zemâm	= *reins*		*and boxing ring*

BIBLIOGRAPHY

(a) BACKGROUND

Sir PERCY SYKES. *A History of Persia* (3rd edition, 2 vols, 1930). The standard history.

E. G. BROWNE. *Literary History of Persia* (4 vols., 1924). Covers the whole ground of Iranian literature.

R. LEVY. *Persian Literature* (in the " World's Manuals " series). A useful handbook.

B. A. DONALDSON. *The Wild Rue* (1938). An interesting study of Iranian folklore.

G. H. EBTEHAJ. *Guidebook on Iran* (Tehran, 1935). Full of information.

L. LOCKHART. *Famous Cities of Iran* (1939). Interesting accounts of the chief Iranian cities.

W. V. EMANUEL. *The Wild Asses* (1939). Light but observant account of a student party's visit to Iran.

FREYA STARK. *The Valleys of the Assassins.* Travels in the more primitive parts.

M. C. COOPER. *Grass* (1925). Picturesque account of the Bakhtiyâri nomads.

J. W. WILLIAMSON. *In a Persian Oilfield* (1927). Description of the operations of the A.I.O.C.
The relevant chapters in :—

H. A. R. GIBB (editor). *Whither Islam ?* (1932).

RUTH W. WOODSMALL. *Moslem Women Enter a New World* (1936).

(b) LANGUAGE

W. ST. CLAIR TISDALL. *Modern Persian Conversation Grammar.* In the Otto-Gaspey-Sauer series.

SALEMANN and SHUKOVSKY. *Persische Grammatik* (Berlin, 1889).

Dialects

ARTHUR CHRISTENSEN. *Contributions à la Dialectologie Iranienne* (Copenhagen, 1930, 1935).

D. L. R. LORIMER. *The Phonology of the Bakhtiari ... Dialects* (1922).

OSKAR MANN. *Kurdisch-Persische Forschungen* (Berlin, 1909–1910).

A. K. S. LAMBTON. *Three Persian Dialects* (1938).

Dictionaries

PALMER. *Persian-English Dictionary.*

—— *English-Persian Dictionary.*

STEINGASS. *Persian-English Dictionary* (1930).

S. HAIM. *Persian-English Dictionary* (Tehran, 1934–36, 2 vols.)

—— *English-Persian Dictionary* (Tehran, 1930–31, 2 vols.).